Kalamazoo Outdoor Gourmet, LLC

11 South LaSalle Street
Fifth Floor
Chicago, IL 60603

1.800.868.1699

www.KalamazooGourmet.com

Cook:Out

FRESH INGREDIENTS   FRESH AIR   FRESH FLAVORS FROM THE GRILL

Acknowledgments

Many thanks to Kalamazoo Outdoor Gourmet. What better role could I ask for in a company? As if leading product development for such an outstanding line of cooking equipment wasn't enough, I also have the opportunity for creative expression through food. Without Kalamazoo Outdoor Gourmet, this cookbook would not be possible.

To my son Alex, who shows up with a new and incredible Lego® creation he wants photographed every time he sees pictures of food being shot.

To my lovely wife Kate, official taste tester for all recipes, good and bad.

To my parents, always supportive, who encouraged me to cook at an early age.

And, last but not least, to Jen, Polly and Chris at Kalamazoo Outdoor Gourmet, whose editing made some sort of sense out of these recipes.

Cook:Out

The grill is at the heart of so many great flavors it is no wonder people who love good food are doing more of their cooking outdoors. The perfect dry and searing heat of a charcoal fire or the smoky flavors of orchard woods are in their element. The flavors are bigger. The environment more enjoyable. The pride of tending the fire more rewarding.

This cookbook collects the best recipes from the popular Kalamazoo Outdoor Gourmet newsletter and GourmetPatio.com blog, plus quite a few tasty extras never before published. Some of the recipes are new versions of old standards, like the Dry-Rubbed Barbecue Chicken. Some are entirely untraditional, like the Grilled Red Grapes with Dark Chocolate Honey Sauce. All represent a commitment to cooking with fresh ingredients and bringing great dining experiences home with a casual flair.

I hope you enjoy preparing the food in this book as much as I do. Take pride in your cooking and have fun doing it!

Table of Contents

Outdoor Cooking Techniques

Gas, Charcoal or Wood Cooking Which is best? This question cannot be answered easily, perhaps not at all. We can, however, describe the differences. A charcoal fire produces a drier heat than a gas fire, which produces more water vapor in the fire. Contrary to popular myth, a charcoal fire has no flavor. Any flavor that was in the wood was burned out in the kiln used to produce the charcoal. It is the dry heat characteristic that helps create the desirable "crust" outside a perfectly cooked steak.

Grilling or roasting with a wood fire is my favorite way to cook. A wood fire can produce a drier heat, similar to a charcoal fire, but there is still a little flavor left in the fire. Similar to working with charcoal, you should not grill over a wood fire until the fire has settled down. The wood chunks should be somewhat ashed over and glowing red. A wood fire will not last as long in this state as a charcoal fire will.

A gas fire offers more convenience than wood or charcoal cooking, and the food can indeed taste great. The whole experience is a little cleaner and a little less time consuming but, perhaps, also a little less fun.

Hybrid Cooking A hybrid grill combines the best of all worlds — gas, charcoal *and* wood. This grill offers the convenience of a gas grill while still delivering the cooking experiences of a charcoal grill. Perhaps best of all, a hybrid grill consumes less charcoal or wood thanks to the ability of the gas burners to supplement the heat.

Direct Grilling The most common type of outdoor cooking, direct grilling, places the food on the grill grate *directly* above the fire. The food is cooked for a relatively short period of time, usually less than 20 minutes. The temperatures used typically range between 350° and 600°F, and the technique is generally appropriate for food that is less than 2 inches in thickness. Direct grilling is used for delicious steaks, fish fillets, burgers, chops, chicken breasts and vegetables.

For those perfect grill marks we all love, the food should only be flipped once, about halfway through the grilling time. This gives time for the grill grate to leave its mark. For a crosshatch pattern, rotate the food between 60 and 90 degrees halfway through cooking each side. The food will still be turned over only once, but it also will be rotated once while cooking each side.

How do you know what the temperature is at the grilling surface? The hood thermometer won't tell you, but there is a pretty reliable technique you can use: Place your open hand, palm-down, a few inches above the grill grate and count the number of seconds before the heat becomes too uncomfortable. For most people, pulling your hand away after about six seconds will equate to 400°F. Five seconds is usually about 500°F, the most common grilling temperature in this book, and the equivalent to four seconds is about 600°F.

Finally, a note on sticking food: First, make sure the grill grate is hot and clean; second, oil the food and not the grate; third, be patient. Most foods, especially fish, will release from the grate when it is time to flip. I prefer to use tongs for turning almost everything except burgers and some fish fillets. Lifting food away from the surface is often easier than scraping it off the surface with a turner.

Indirect Grilling Indirect grilling places the food next to the fire rather than above the fire. This technique is used for larger foods with longer cooking times, typically more than 20 minutes. Turkeys, prime rib, whole chickens, racks of lamb and large chops are all ideal for roasting on the grill using the indirect grilling technique.

While roasting food, the grill hood should remain closed as much as possible, and you should be able to rely on the hood thermometer for accurate cooking temperature readings. Using wood smoke with roasting techniques is called "smoke roasting," and this can add fabulous flavor. Read on for different options for adding smoke to your grilling.

For gas grills, preheat the entire grill and then turn some of the burners off for the indirect zone before putting the food on the grill.

Searing Searing is a type of direct grilling using more extreme heat. A grill must be able to reach at least 700°F for good searing. Searing is done quickly and is often followed by continued cooking at lower temperatures. Some gas grills feature dedicated searing zones, usually with an infrared burner. Searing temperatures are also easily reached over charcoal or wood fires.

Barbecue Barbecue sauce does not make barbecue. Low heat and long cooking times with the use of wood smoke are the key characteristics. Temperatures as low as 200°F are used for as long as 24 hours. The food is kept away from the fire by using the indirect grilling technique or even an offset fire box.

Barbecue techniques are best for meats that would otherwise be undesirable or a tough cut, such as beef brisket. The longer cooking times and lower temperatures will render the fat into the muscle to deliver more tender results. One hallmark of good barbecue is the "smoke ring," an outer pink layer that penetrates the meat as a result of the smoking process. Barbecued pork ribs should be penetrated all the way through. Pink ribs are not undercooked — actually, they are perfectly smoked.

Spit Roasting or Rotisserie Food roasted on a spit bastes in its own juices. The only difference between roasting and rotisserie cooking is the use of the spinning spit. Rotisserie is generally done with indirect heat, next to the fire, but can be done directly above the fire.

Most food that is typically cooked on a rotisserie, such as whole chickens or turkeys, can also be cooked with indirect grilling techniques.

Smoking The most effective traditional smoking is done on a dedicated smoker, which will normally have a fire box offset from the smoking chamber where the food goes. However, wood smoke flavor can be added to food cooked on a grill in a number of ways. When using smoke on a grill, keep the hood closed as much as possible and give the smoke time to permeate the food.

Charcoal or Hybrid Grill Wet wood chips can be scattered over a charcoal fire once the coals are ashed over and ready for cooking. Smoke can be produced in this manner for both direct and indirect grilling techniques.

Gas Grill Smoker Tray Many gas grills have a smoker tray above one of the burners. Wet wood chips are placed in the smoker tray, which produces smoke for use with indirect grilling techniques.

Foil Smoking Envelopes A convenient way to produce smoke for indirect grilling or smoke roasting is through the use of foil smoking envelopes. A layer of dry wood chips under a layer of wet wood chips is folded into a foil envelope and sealed. Holes are pierced with a fork to allow smoke to escape without providing so much oxygen that the wood bursts into flames.

Multiple smoking envelopes can be used for longer cooking sessions. Once an envelope is spent, simply replace it with another. Smoking envelopes can be placed directly on the grill grate, on the heat diffusers of a gas grill, or on a bed of ashed-over charcoal.

Cooking Pizzas The best way to cook pizza is on a high-quality pizza stone. Of course, you can cook pizza in a pizza oven, but you can also do it perfectly on the grill. Simply preheat the pizza stone in the indirect grilling zone of the grill for an hour, usually at a temperature of 500°F. Bake the pizza with the crust directly on the stone, with the hood closed, until done.

To cook a pizza directly on the grill grate, place the rolled-out or tossed dough over the fire for direct grilling. After a minute or two, flip the crust with tongs and add the toppings on the grilled side, being sure not to overload the pizza. Close the grill hood and continue cooking until the toppings are melted.

A great benefit of having a pizza oven in addition to the grill is that you can use them at the same time. With a pizza stone on the grill, use of the grill is limited. With both a pizza oven and a grill available, you can prepare appetizer pizzas in the oven while roasting whole chickens on the grill for the entree.

Grilling Basics: Grilling Better

A few key skills make grilling more satisfying and successful. The following tips and tricks represent some of the best of what I have learned from cooking with fire over the years.

Whole Chicken More than rotisserie, "Beer Can" or other popular methods for cooking a whole chicken, I prefer to butterfly and roast it. Butterflying a chicken (also called spatchcock) lays the bird flat for quicker and more even cooking. A butterflied chicken can be cooked at higher temperatures, so you are able to more easily achieve a nice, crispy skin and perfectly cooked meat. Whether using a barbecue rub or simply brushing the bird with olive oil, this is my favorite way to prepare chicken. It takes about 35 minutes for a whole fryer laid directly on the grill grate in the indirect cooking zone at 500°F. I remove the bird when the juices from a prick in the thigh meat run clear or when an instant-read meat thermometer reads 170°F. (The USDA recommends 180°F. See page 162 for a complete Food Temperature Chart.)

To butterfly a chicken, use kitchen shears to cut out the backbone and discard it. Without cutting through the breast meat, snip the breast bone part way down the middle from the top. Open the chicken out flat with the skin-side-up. The thighs should point in toward the middle with the drumsticks pointing out the back. Tuck the wings up and under as shown in the photo at left.

Chicken Breasts The challenge with cooking a boneless chicken breast perfectly is the shape: thick at one end and pointed at the other. For even grilling, a "palliard," which flattens the breast to a uniform thickness, will yield juicy and tender results throughout. Place the breast between two layers of heavy plastic (I split open a zip-top freezer bag and place it between the layers) and then pound it to about 1/2-inch thick. Brush each breast with olive oil, sprinkle with salt and grill directly over a hot fire for a few minutes per side until cooked through but still juicy and tender.

Burgers First, try to select USDA Choice grade beef. Choice ground round is my favorite way to go, and I think it improves the quality of a burger far more than it increases the price. Ground round is delivered to most markets in a tube-shaped plastic bag. Ask the butcher to cut off 1-inch-thick slices, creating patties that are about ½ pound each. This is the perfect thickness and weight for the grill, and I think the lack of handling helps with the texture. Forming the patties rather than slicing them can lead to overworking the burgers, and they can end up a little tough.

Chef Bobby Flay offers a tip to compensate for the way a juicy burger plumps up on the grill. By recessing the patty in the middle before cooking, the burger becomes flat when it plumps up. Just use your fingers to recess the middle of each patty a bit from both sides.

The next step in a perfect burger is to brush it with olive oil. This helps form the flavorful crust that I think is one of the hallmarks of a great burger. Grill the burgers directly over a medium-hot fire (about 450°F), turning only once, until it is cooked to the desired doneness. When cooking for larger parties, it can be a good idea to cook an extra, sacrificial burger. Break into this burger a couple of minutes before you expect the burgers to be cooked to medium to check your timing. Continue cooking to at least medium-well, an internal temperature of 160°F.

Skirt Steak Skirt steak should be cooked quickly over a hot fire to medium doneness — no more, no less. I like to first squeeze a lime over the steak, then brush it with olive oil, sprinkle it with salt and toss it over a wood fire. When prepared properly, skirt steak is tender and full of flavor. After letting it rest a few minutes, slice skirt steak across the grain to compensate for its stringy character.

Filet Mignon My favorite way to cook filet is to sear it directly over a hot wood fire and then move it to an indirect cooking zone, close the hood and let it coast up to temperature for 15 to 20 minutes. This creates a nicely browned exterior crust and a tender, juicy center. As with all steaks, I lightly oil and salt the filets before they hit the grill. The searing is done at about 700°F, and the indirect time is spent at about 500°F. This turns each filet into a miniature tenderloin roast.

Ribeye or New York Strip   Ribeye steaks up to 1½ inches thick and New York strip (or sirloin) steaks up to 2 inches thick are best cooked directly over the fire. Thicker ribeyes should spend a couple of minutes per side over the fire, then move them to an indirect zone to coast up to temperature with the hood closed.

For direct grilling to perfection, lightly oil and salt the steaks and them place them over the hot fire. After a quarter of the total cooking time, rotate them a quarter-turn to crosshatch the grill marks. After half the cooking time, flip them over, and then rotate them another quarter-turn when they are ¾ done. I prefer not to handle the steaks any more than this, which requires a good sense of the cooking time before you start. Get to know your grill well and you will be better able to predict the total cooking time based on the thickness and the cut of the steak. As a starting point, a strip steak 1½ inches thick will be cooked to medium-rare after about 12 minutes over a hot fire.

For both types of steak, let them rest for 3 to 5 minutes after coming off the grill before cutting into them.

Pork Chops   My favorite way to cook chops is super-thick and with the bone. A 3-inch-thick chop can be seared over direct heat for a minute or two and then get smoke-roasted for up to 30 minutes at 500°F. For the juiciest chops, try brining them before cooking. As with steaks, I suggest a light brushing with olive oil and a little salt before the chops go onto the grill.

Salmon   Salmon is one of the most popular fishes on the grill. I prefer fillets to steaks, so that is the cut we'll walk through. Squeeze a little lemon over the fillets, brush them with olive oil and sprinkle with salt. Cook them in the direct cooking zone at 500°F with the skin-side up. When the fish starts to draw up away from the surface at the edges and the skin is pulling flat across the top, it is time to turn them over. This usually takes 6 to 8 minutes. Continue cooking with the skin-side down until the fish flakes cleanly under gentle pressure. When done, you can slide the turner between the meat and the skin, removing the meat and leaving the skin behind on the grill.

Shrimp   The secret to great grilled shrimp is great big shrimp. For the grill, the bigger the better. Devein the shrimp with a slit down the back that also partially butterflies the shrimp. Grill over medium-high direct heat, turning once, until the flesh in the slit turns opaque. Remove from the grill immediately.

Asparagus or Green Beans   Grilled green vegetables make a great side dish. The technique for grilling green beans and asparagus is the same, and the secret is to use a little lemon juice.

Toss cleaned and trimmed asparagus or green beans with equal parts lemon juice and olive oil. If your grill grate is not like the Kalamazoo Outdoor Gourmet vegetable surface — sized so that the veggies won't fall down into the fire — use a preheated grill basket over a direct fire with a grilling temperature of 500°F. Remove the vegetables from the oil and lemon mixture and put them in the direct grilling zone, being careful not to drop too much oil into the grill. Toss them around on the grill until nicely marked, then remove them while still crisp. Season with a little salt and serve them quickly.

Peach Bourbon Habañero Hot Wings

With the exception of a perfectly-executed classic Buffalo wing, I most enjoy a hot wing that brings together sweetness and spice. That is why we are teaming up peaches and Habañero. Bourbon joins the roster to add a layer of complexity.

Serves 10

For the Blue Cheese Dressing

3/4 cup mayonnaise

1/4 cup sour cream

3/4 cup coarsely crumbled blue cheese

1/2 teaspoon fresh lemon zest

1/2 teaspoon coarse-ground black pepper

For the Marinade

1/2 cup hot sauce (I use Cholula)

1/2 cup freshly-squeezed lemon juice

1/4 cup canola oil

8 cloves fresh garlic, crushed

3 tablespoons soy sauce

40 chicken wing halves (about 4 to 4½ pounds)

For the Peach Bourbon Habañero Glaze

1/2 cup unsalted butter

1 cup peach preserves

2 tablespoons light-brown sugar

4 fresh habañero peppers, quartered (wear surgical-type gloves to protect your hands)

1/4 cup bourbon (I use Knob Creek)

1 cup wood chips (optional), soaked in water for at least 1 hour

Celery ribs (optional), however many you like, cut lengthwise into 2 or 3 pieces and then crosswise into 3 to 4-inch sticks

Directions

The dressing can be made up to 24 hours ahead. Combine the mayonnaise, sour cream, lemon rind and pepper in a bowl. Stir in blue cheese until well mixed. If the mixture is too thick, stir in buttermilk, a small amount at a time, until you like the consistency. Cover and store in the refrigerator until serving.

Whisk together all marinade ingredients (except the chicken) in a large glass mixing bowl. Rinse the wings under cold, running water and dry with paper towels. Add the wings to the marinade and stir to thoroughly coat all the wings. Cover and refrigerate. The wings should marinate in the refrigerator for 4 to 12 hours, whatever timing is most convenient. Turn the wings occasionally to ensure they are well-marinated.

Preheat the grill for indirect cooking at 400° to 500°F. If you are using wood chips, get them smoking. For gas grills, I find it easiest to use a quick smoking envelope.

While the grill is heating and smoke is starting, prepare the glaze. In a medium saucepan, melt the butter over low heat. Add the preserves, brown sugar and habañero, stirring constantly until the preserves have melted. Stir in the bourbon and keep warm over very low heat until you are ready to baste. Keep an eye on the pot because the sugars can easily caramelize or burn.

Put the wings on the grill in the indirect cooking zone. Discard the marinade. Cook the wings with the lid closed and the grill at 400° to 500°F. Turn the wings every 5 minutes until the skin is golden brown and starting to turn crisp, about 20 to 25 minutes. Baste the wings and continue grilling for about 10 more minutes, basting lightly every 2 minutes. If the basted wings are not caramelizing over indirect heat, move to direct heat for no more than the final 2 minutes. Serve the wings with blue cheese dressing and celery sticks.

Note: As written, I would describe these wings as "medium" hot. You can prepare them with varying degrees of spiciness, depending on the hot sauce you use in the marinade and the number of habañeros in the glaze. Whether or not you discard the seeds and ribs from the peppers will also have a big influence on the heat.

Asian Citrus Hot Wings

I really enjoy a dish that balances the key components of sweet, savory, tart and spicy. That's what these wings are all about. Honey provides the sweet, citrus offers the tang, soy sauce is the savory component, and habañero chiles bring the heat. How much heat is up to you. I would describe this recipe as mild, so if you want it hotter, use more chiles and leave them in the sauce longer.

Serves 4 to 6

For the Quick Marinade

1/4 cup soy sauce

1/4 cup extra virgin olive oil

2 tablespoons fresh lime juice

20 chicken wing "drummettes"

For the Asian Citrus Glaze

1/2 cup freshly squeezed lime juice

1/6 cup soy sauce

1/2 cup freshly squeezed orange juice

2/3 cup honey

2 habañero chiles, quartered

For Garnish

1 to 2 tablespoons thinly sliced green onion

Directions

Prepare the grill for direct cooking at 400° to 500°F.

Use a fork to whisk together the marinade ingredients in a large bowl. Add the "drummettes" and toss to coat. Let rest at room temperature for about 20 minutes while you prepare the glaze.

Measure the lime juice in a measuring cup, then add the soy sauce to fill to the 2/3 cup mark (for 1/6 cup soy sauce). Transfer to a sauce pan, add the orange juice and bring to a boil over medium heat. Simmer, stirring occasionally until reduced and thickened, about 20 minutes. Be careful not to burn the reduction. Stir in a little more than half of the honey and add the chiles. Simmer the chiles in the glaze for about 3 minutes, stirring occasionally. Test for spiciness along the way. Add more honey as needed to balance the flavor. When the glaze has the right amount of bite, remove the habañero pieces. Reduce the heat to very low to keep the glaze warm while you grill the chicken. Be very careful not to burn the glaze now that the honey has been added.

Discard the marinade from the wings. Grill the wings over direct heat, turning occasionally until the skin is crispy and browned and the meat is almost cooked through, about 15 minutes.

Reserve about a quarter of the glaze. Baste half of the remaining glaze over the wings. Continue grilling for 2 minutes. Turn the wings, baste again, and continue grilling for 3 minutes more.

Remove the wings from the grill and toss with the reserved glaze. Transfer to a platter and sprinkle the green onion over the top.

Tip: Sauces or glazes with a high sugar content like this one should normally only be used for the final few minutes of grilling because the sugars will cause the glaze to burn. Keep a close eye on the grill and keep the food moving to avoid excessive burning.

Tequila Barbecue Chicken Kebabs

Our quick and easy Tequila Barbecue Sauce lends robust flavor to these chicken kebabs. Make a little extra sauce if you want to try it in other dishes.

Serves 6

2 cups Tequila Barbecue Sauce (recipe follows)

1½ pounds boneless, skinless chicken breasts

3 red bell peppers (or use 1½ red and 1½ orange for added color), cleaned and cut into squares

2 poblano chiles, cleaned and cut into squares

2 ears corn on the cob, shucked and cut into 1-inch pieces

1 red onion, cut into squares

6 skewers, about 8 inches long

Tequila Barbecue Sauce

1 cup ketchup

6 tablespoons pomegranate molasses (look for it in the aisle with Asian specialty ingredients)

1 cup light-brown sugar

2 teaspoons hot sauce

1 cup tequila

8 cloves garlic, crushed

Combine all ingredients. Yields about 2 cups. Store in a covered container in the refrigerator.

Directions

Cut the chicken into large cubes for the kebabs and place them in a zip-top freezer bag with 1 cup of tequila barbecue sauce. Remove as much air as possible, seal and refrigerate for 2 to 4 hours.

When it is time to prepare for cooking, get the grill ready for direct grilling at about 500°F.

Assemble the kebabs, alternating between chicken, bell peppers, poblanos, corn and red onion.

Grill the kebabs over direct heat for a few minutes per side, brushing with the reserved 1 cup of barbecue sauce each time you turn them. The chicken should be cooked through in about 15 minutes. Be careful not to slop too much barbecue sauce onto the grill while you baste because the sugars will burn quickly.

Serve hot.

Note: A lot of companies are offering nice grilling tools these days, including some pretty fancy skewers for kebabs. Some are forged stainless steel and some have "pusher" disks to help you transfer the kebab bits to your plate without getting your fingers dirty.

The most important skewer design feature, in my opinion, is a flat blade. A flat blade will help keep the pieces of food from rotating on the kebab. The blade doesn't have to be very wide to do this, just markedly wider than it is thick (see the skewers in the picture on the left).

When the piece of food can rotate on the skewer, it is harder to turn the skewer for even cooking. Worse yet, when some of the pieces are rotating and some are not, you have to realign them over and over or totally forget about even cooking. A flat blade will keep all the food aligned so that you can easily cook everything evenly with a few turns of the skewer.

I've tried several different types of flat bamboo skewers for cooking. All of them work well. Some have double prongs, which make for a nice presentation. If you can't find flat bamboo skewers, you can use pairs of round skewers in parallel to accomplish the same thing. Bamboo skewers can be soaked for an our before use to help prevent them from burning on the grill. You can also lay a folded strip of aluminum foil on the grill grate underneath exposed skewer ends to protect them.

Dry-Rubbed Barbecue Chicken

You can slave for hours making barbecued chicken at 230°F, or you can grill-roast this quick version your guests will love. By butterflying the chicken and quickly roasting with wood smoke at 500°F, you will have tender, juicy and flavorful chicken ready to serve in just 35 minutes. By using a dry barbecue rub and no sauce, this chicken is also easier to eat without making a mess.

Serves 8 to 12

1/2 cup Not-So-Basic Barbecue Rub (recipe follows)

1/2 cup light-brown sugar

3 whole fryer chickens, butterflied (see page 7 for instructions)

1 cup hickory wood chips, soaked for 1 hour

Not-So-Basic Barbecue Rub

1/4 cup kosher salt

1/4 cup light-brown sugar

1/4 cup demerara or turbinado sugar

1 tablespoon smoked paprika

2 teaspoons ground cinnamon

1½ teaspoons chipotle chili powder

1½ teaspoons grated nutmeg

1 teaspoon ground allspice

1 teaspoon freshly ground black pepper

1/2 teaspoon ground cayenne pepper

1/4 teaspoon ground cloves

Combine all ingredients. Yields 1+ cup. Store any extra in an air-tight container in the refrigerator for up to 3 months.

Directions

Prepare the grill for indirect grilling at 500°F with wood smoke using hickory chips (or your favorite wood variety).

Combine the Not-So-Basic Barbecue Rub and the brown sugar. Rub onto both sides of the chickens.

Place the chickens flat on the grill in the indirect zone with the skin-sides up. (If your grill is not as large as a Kalamazoo 900 Series, you will likely need to cook the chickens only one or two at a time.)

Cook the chickens, without turning them over, until the internal temperature of the thigh measures 165° to 175°F. On a Kalamazoo, this should take only 35 minutes. Check the chickens after 20 minutes in case they need to be rearranged on the cooking surface relative to the heat source for more even cooking.

Remove the chickens from the grill and let rest for a few minutes. Quarter and serve.

Variations on the Not-So-Basic Barbecue Rub This rub is a great base for a variety of uses. For a more traditional barbecue flavor, add brown sugar as I have for this chicken recipe. For a more pungent and spicy approach, mix it with cracked black pepper. For East-meets-West barbecue flavor, mix in equal parts Madras curry powder and brown sugar.

The rub is also used in the Coffee-Rubbed Beef Back Ribs (page 27), the Hearty Winter Chili (page 39), the Barbecue Shrimp Skewers with Peach Salsa (page 67) and the Creamed Corn Fresca (page 111).

Balsamic Barbecue Chicken and Glazed Potatoes

There are many recipes with variations on Balsamic Barbecue Sauce, but ours goes beyond simply adding balsamic vinegar to a basic barbecue sauce. Balsamic vinegar is the true core of this sauce, and the results are fantastic. The complex flavors of the vinegar are first sweetened and concentrated by reducing it with honey. After thickening our glaze with a little tomato paste and brown sugar, we add a touch of hot sauce. The delicious mixture, once kissed by the fire of the grill, caramelizes on the chicken for a delightfully layered set of flavors.

Serves 4

For the Balsamic Barbecue Chicken

1/2 cup Balsamic Honey Reduction (recipe follows)

1/4 cup olive oil

4 cloves garlic, crushed

1 whole fryer chicken, quartered

2 tablespoons light-brown sugar

1 tablespoon tomato paste

1/2 teaspoon hot sauce

For the Glazed Potatoes

1/4 cup Balsamic Honey Reduction

1/4 cup olive oil

6 cloves garlic, crushed

6 medium Yukon gold potatoes, halved

Coarse sea salt

Balsamic Honey Reduction

2 cups balsamic vinegar

1/2 cup honey

Combine ingredients in a shallow (preferably nonstick) pan; a large surface area will help speed the evaporation and reduction. Cook the mixture over medium heat, stirring frequently, until reduced to 1 cup. Keep a close eye on it towards the end to avoid burning.

Directions

Balsamic Barbecue Chicken Whisk together 1/4 cup Balsamic Honey Reduction with the olive oil and garlic. Place the chicken quarters in a zip-top plastic bag together with the balsamic mixture, seal and marinate in the refrigerator for 2 to 4 hours.

Prepare the grill for indirect grilling at about 500°F.

To create the Balsamic Barbecue Sauce, whisk together 1/4 cup Balsamic Honey Reduction with the light-brown sugar, tomato paste and your favorite hot sauce. I use Tabasco.

Remove the chicken quarters from the marinade and discard the marinade. Place the chicken in the indirect cooking zone skin-side up. Baste with Balsamic Barbecue Sauce, close the grill hood and cook with indirect heat for 20 minutes.

After 20 minutes, baste the chicken with more sauce and rotate the pieces (without flipping them over) for even cooking. Close the hood again and cook for 5 to 10 minutes more. The chicken is done when you pierce the meaty part of the thigh and the juices run clear — or when a meat thermometer registers 170°F.

Glazed Potatoes Whisk together the Balsamic Honey Reduction with the olive oil and garlic. Place the potato halves in a zip-top plastic bag, seal and marinate in the refrigerator for 2 to 4 hours.

Prepare the grill for indirect grilling at about 500°F.

Place the potato halves skin-side up in the indirect cooking zone, discarding whatever marinade remains. Close the grill hood and cook with indirect heat for about 30 minutes.

Remove from the grill, sprinkle with sea salt and serve.

Chicken Satay

This Thai restaurant staple is so easy to prepare on the grill that this recipe may become part of your standard entertaining arsenal.

Serves 4 to 6 as an appetizer

1 cup plain yogurt

1 tablespoon freshly grated ginger

2 tablespoons red curry paste

1 teaspoon sriracha (Thai hot sauce)

2 pounds boneless, skinless chicken breasts (about 4 breast halves)

Chopped fresh cilantro

1 jar Thai peanut sauce for satay

Fine sea salt (optional)

24 to 32 flat skewers (see skewer notes on page 15)

Directions

Combine the first four ingredients in a large bowl to create the marinade.

Slice the chicken breasts into thin strips, about 6 to 8 strips per breast half. Toss the strips into the marinade, cover and refrigerate for 2 hours.

Prepare the grill for direct cooking at about 400°F.

Remove the chicken from the marinade and thread the strips onto the water-soaked skewers. Discard the marinade. Let the chicken skewers rise to room temperature for about 10 minutes before grilling. This will help prevent the chicken from sticking to the grill, as it would if it were cold from the refrigerator.

Grill the chicken skewers over direct heat, turning once, until cooked through, about 5 minutes per side. Remove from the grill and test the chicken for taste. Sprinkle with a pinch of fine sea salt if needed.

Transfer to a platter, sprinkle with some chopped cilantro and serve with peanut sauce for dipping.

Apple-Brined Turkey

I am convinced that brining and smoke-roasting the holiday turkey on the grill is the best way to go. Brining adds moisture to food prior to grilling, which can be particularly beneficial for turkey breast because it has so little interior fat. The primary ingredients in a traditional brine are water and salt. The salt helps the muscle cells to bond with water and aids in drawing any other flavors along with it. Apple cider turns up the flavor a notch and is a perfect complement to traditional stuffing.

Serves 12 to 14

12 pound turkey, fresh or thawed

For the Brining Solution

1 gallon unsweetened apple cider

1 cup kosher salt

2/3 cup light-brown sugar

2 tablespoons candied ginger pieces

1 tablespoon whole black peppercorns

2 teaspoons allspice berries, cracked

6 whole cloves

3 star anise

1 gallon ice-cold water

1 orange, quartered

2 brining bags

For Roasting the Turkey

4 cups apple wood chips

1 sweet onion, quartered

1 baking apple, quartered

1 cinnamon stick

Canola oil for brushing the turkey

Foil turkey pan and roasting rack

Cotton string and 1 bamboo skewer

1 cup water

Directions

Brining the Turkey Combine 1/2 gallon of apple cider with all other brine ingredients, except the water and oranges, in a large stock pot and bring to a boil, stirring until all of the sugar and salt are completely dissolved. Remove from heat.

Stir in the remaining apple cider and the ice water. Place the brine in the refrigerator to cool if necessary.

Discard the giblets and neck from the turkey. Rinse and pat dry. Place the quartered orange in the cavity. Place one brining bag inside the other. Working in a large roasting pan or a clean sink, place the turkey inside the inner bag breast-side-down and then fill with the brining solution. Squeeze out all the air and seal the bags, one inside the other, ensuring the turkey is completely submerged. I place the bagged turkey inside a large stock pot to help keep the turkey fully submerged.

Brine the turkey in the refrigerator overnight.

Roasting the Turkey Soak half of the applewood chips in water for at least 1 hour. Prepare a grill for indirect cooking between 275° and 325°F. When the grill is ready, add some of the soaked wood chips to the grill (learn about smoking techniques on page 5 or at *KalamazooGourmet.com*).

Remove the turkey from the brine and pat thoroughly dry with paper towel. Place the onion, apple and cinnamon stick inside the cavity, then tie the legs together with a cotton string. Pull the skin over the neck opening and secure with a small skewer. Set the turkey on a roasting rack inside a heavy-gauge foil pan. Brush turkey lightly with oil.

Set the turkey in the pan on the cooking grate in the indirect cooking zone. Pour 1 cup water into the pan. Close the grill and cook over medium heat. To maintain an even temperature with a charcoal grill, add more charcoal regularly (usually a few pieces every half hour or so). Continue adding wood chips as desired.

Check the turkey periodically, you may want to cover the wing tips and/or the whole turkey to prevent the skin from getting too brown. The turkey is done when its juices run clear and the internal temperature of the thickest part of the thigh is about 170°F. Estimate about 12 to 14 minutes per pound, typically 2½ to 3 hours. Remove the turkey from the grill, cover loosely with foil and let stand 15 minutes. (The temperature will rise 5° to 10°F as the turkey rests.) Carve the turkey and serve on a warm platter.

Find the recipe for sausage-stuffed sweet potatoes at KalamazooGourmet.com.

Blue Cheese-Stuffed Blackened Turkey Breast with Cajun Corn "Gravy"

Turkey is a great match for bold flavors, and they don't get any bolder than these. The blackened crust outside the turkey complements the smooth, melted blue cheese inside. The hint of mustard flavor in the "gravy" rounds it all out perfectly. Brining the turkey helps ensure that it comes off the grill juicy and tender.

Serves 4

For the Turkey

1/2 gallon (8 cups) water

1/2 cup kosher salt

1/2 cup light-brown sugar

1 turkey breast half, skin-on, about 2½ pounds

2 large cloves garlic, crushed

Leaves from 1 sprig rosemary, chopped

1/4 cup extra virgin olive oil

2 ounces blue cheese, sliced

Fine sea salt

About 1 tablespoon Chef Paul Prudhomme's Poultry Magic seasoning blend

For the Cajun Corn "Gravy"

2 teaspoons Chef Paul Prudhomme's Poultry Magic seasoning blend

1 teaspoon Colman's mustard powder

1 cup white wine

1 clove garlic, minced or crushed

1/2 shallot, minced

Juice of 1/4 lemon

1/2 cup fresh corn kernels

1/2 cup heavy cream

4 tablespoons unsalted butter

Directions

Create a basic brine by whisking together the water, kosher salt and brown sugar in a very large bowl until dissolved. Place the turkey breast half in the bowl, skin-side down. Cover and refrigerate for 4 hours.

Combine the crushed garlic, rosemary and olive oil in a small bowl and let the flavors blend for at least 1 hour.

Prepare the grill for indirect cooking at 350° to 375°F.

Remove the turkey from the brine and rinse well under cool, running water. Dry thoroughly. Release the skin from one edge of the breast and pull it back. Cut a lengthwise slit in the middle of the breast and stuff it with blue cheese. Pull the skin tightly back over the slit and pin it in place using a couple of toothpicks.

Brush the breast with the reserved flavored olive oil and sprinkle with sea salt. Sprinkle the skin generously with Chef Paul Prudhomme's Poultry Magic. This will form the blackened crust.

Place the prepared breast in the indirect cooking zone with the skin-side up and cook with the hood closed for approximately 45 minutes to 1 hour. The turkey is cooked when an instant-read thermometer inserted in the meatiest part of the breast (away from the blue cheese stuffing) reads 165° to 170°F (the USDA recommends 180°F).

Mix the remaining Poultry Magic seasoning blend with the mustard powder in a small dish to eliminate all lumps. Reserve.

Combine the wine, garlic, shallot and lemon juice in a medium skillet. Boil over medium heat, stirring constantly until reduced to about 1/4 cup. Force the reduced mixture through a mesh strainer and return the liquid to the saucepan. Add 1 teaspoon of the garlic and shallot back into the saucepan and discard the rest. Add the corn, cream, reserved spice blend and mustard powder, then bring to a simmer, stirring constantly.

Remove from heat and transfer to a blender. Blend until as smooth as possible. At this point, you can cover and refrigerate the mixture for an hour or two. To finish the "gravy," return the corn and cream mixture to the skillet just before serving and bring to a simmer over low heat. Whisk in the butter one tablespoon at a time. Do not allow to boil. Move the skillet off the heat if necessary.

To serve the turkey, first remove the toothpicks. Slice the breast into 1-inch-thick pieces. Drizzle the Cajun Corn "Gravy" onto each plate and place the sliced turkey on top.

Coffee-Rubbed Beef Back Ribs

Our Quick and Aromatic Barbecue Ribs recipe (page 59) makes great pork ribs in about 2½ hours, much less time than the traditional approach.

Here, we're making some great beef ribs in just 30 to 40 minutes. Done right, they will have the texture of a nice ribeye steak — we're not looking for "fall-off-the-bone tender" ribs but something meatier. A barbecue rub with ground coffee gives the ribs an earthy barbecue flavor.

Serves 4 to 6

1/4 cup Not-So-Basic Barbecue Rub (see recipe on page 17)

1/2 cup light-brown sugar

1 tablespoon ground coffee (I suggest finely-ground Illy dark roast coffee for espresso)

2 racks of beef back ribs, 7 to 8 bones each

Extra virgin olive oil

Directions

Combine the first 3 ingredients to create the coffee barbecue rub.

Prepare a grill for direct grilling at 375°F to 400°F. A charcoal fire is preferred. You'll know the fire is at the right temp when you hold your hand, palm-down, a couple of inches above the grill grate for a 6 to 7-second count before needing to pull it away from the heat.

If the butcher hasn't already done it for you, remove the membrane from the bone-side of the ribs. You may also want to cut each rack into 2 parts for easier handling on the grill. Dry the ribs with paper towels and then lightly brush on both sides with olive oil. Sprinkle the bone sides of the ribs with a moderate amount of coffee barbecue rub and work it in with your fingers. Spread a generous amount of the rub onto the meat side and massage that in as well. Let the seasoned ribs rest for about 20 minutes.

Place the seasoned ribs on the grill directly above the fire with the bone side down. Close the grill hood and cook for 20 minutes, rotating the ribs as needed for even cooking. Turn the ribs over to put the meat side down. Close the hood and continue cooking for 10 to 20 minutes more. Again, rotate the ribs occasionally for even cooking.

Keep an eye out for burning rub. The surface of the ribs should remain a rich, mahogany color and should not turn black. With a charcoal fire, the dying heat is good for this stage of the cooking. For a gas fire, you may wish to turn the heat down slightly during the second half of the cooking.

When done, the ribs should be bubbling as the fat is rendered away, and the rub should have turned into a nice crust. If you get it just right, there will be a tree bark-like texture to the outside of the meat.

Remove the ribs from the grill and let them rest for 3 to 5 minutes. Slice the ribs apart and serve separated. When slicing, start at the rib end where only a single bone tip is visible for each rib. Cut toward the other end where you will eventually encounter the chine bone. At this point, jog the knife left or right to continue separating the ribs and work around the chine bone.

Heavenly Burgers

These burgers are so good, you won't need condiments at the table. Ground round is joined by grilled Vidalia onions, fresh guacamole, Monterey Jack cheese, a slice of tomato and grilled garlic buns for a perfect combination of flavors and textures.

Serves 8

3 cloves garlic

1/2 cup extra virgin olive oil

8 golden hamburger buns, split

Hickory or alder-smoked salt

8 patties Choice ground round, 85% lean, 1/2 pound each, 1-inch thick

2 Vidalia onions

3 avocados

2 limes

Small handful cilantro leaves, chopped

Fine sea salt

8 slices Monterey Jack cheese

2 ripe tomatoes, sliced 1/2-inch thick

Directions

A couple of hours before cooking, crush the garlic cloves into about 1/2 cup of olive oil. Let sit at room temperature, stirring once or twice while the garlic infuses the oil.

Prepare the grill for direct cooking at 400° to 500°F.

While the grill is heating, brush some of the garlic-infused olive oil onto the sliced sides of the hamburger buns and then sprinkle with smoked salt.

Recess the centers of the ground round patties (see page 7 for our tips on creating the perfect burger). Brush the patties on both sides with the remaining garlic-infused olive oil and sprinkle with smoked salt.

Slice the onions 3/4-inch thick, stick toothpicks into the sides to keep the rings together and sprinkle with salt.

Cut the avocados in half lengthwise, working around and not cutting through the pit. Remove the pit and scoop out the meat into a large bowl. Mash coarsely. Stir in the juice of 1 to 2 limes, the cilantro and sea salt to taste. Cover guacamole with plastic wrap, pressing the wrap down into the surface to keep oxygen out.

Place the onion slices in a cooler area of the direct grilling zone. Turn after about 7 minutes. Add the burgers directly over the hottest part of the fire after about 3 minutes more. If you have special requests for temperature, start well-done burgers earlier and medium-rare burgers later. For medium burgers, cook for about 12 to 15 minutes total, turning once. When you turn the burgers over, top each with a couple rings of grilled onion and then add a slice of cheese to melt over the top.

As the burgers near completion, add the buns to the grill, cut-side down. Cook until lightly toasted without drying the buns out. Remove the buns from the grill and spread the guacamole onto the bottom half of each. Place the cooked burgers on top of the guacamole. Add a slice of tomato and the top bun to each and serve.

The recipe for Grill-Roasted French Fries with Avocado Aioli is available at KalamazooGourmet.com.

Liberty Burgers

These burgers are inspired by the classic cheese steak sandwiches of Philadelphia – home of the Liberty Bell. Start with choice ground beef, top with provolone cheese, grilled peppers and onions and serve on a toasted Italian roll.

Serves 8

4 pounds Choice ground round, 85% lean, formed into 8 hamburger patties

Extra virgin olive oil

Fine sea salt

8 Italian rolls, sized appropriately for the burgers, split

1 red bell pepper, thinly sliced

1 poblano pepper, thinly sliced

1 banana pepper, thinly sliced

1 Vidalia onion, thinly sliced

8 slices provolone cheese

Directions

Prepare the grill for direct grilling with two temperature zones; one medium-low and one medium-high. Preheat a 12-inch cast iron skillet over the hottest part of the fire.

Recess the centers of the hamburger patties (see page 7 for our tips on creating the perfect burger). Brush the patties all over with olive oil and liberally season with sea salt.

Lightly brush the insides of the rolls with olive oil and lightly season with sea salt.

Toss the peppers and onion with about 1 tablespoon olive oil.

Grill the burgers over the hot zone of the fire, turning once, about 4 minutes per side. Toast the rolls over the cooler zone of the fire during the second half of the burger cooking. Transfer the cooked burgers to a platter, top each with a slice of cheese, and cover with foil to rest and to melt the cheese. Remove the toasted rolls from the fire and reserve.

Cook the peppers and onions in the hot skillet, tossing frequently until nicely browned, about five minutes. Top each burger with peppers and onions, transfer to the rolls and serve.

Teriyaki Burgers with Spicy Broccoli Slaw

The East-meets-West flair of these burgers will delight your guests. By itself, the slaw is intense and spicy on the tongue. On the burgers as a condiment, however, it has just the right zing. The teriyaki caramelizes on the outside of the burgers for a sweet and savory crust. Our plant manager at Kalamazoo Outdoor Gourmet calls these "Forty Dollar Burgers." Try the same teriyaki glaze on grilled salmon, and check out the orange variation on the next page.

Serves 8

For the Spicy Broccoli Slaw

1½ cups peeled and julienned broccoli stems

3/4 cup shredded red cabbage

1/2 cup peeled and shredded or julienned carrots

1/2 red bell pepper, seeded and shaved

1/4 red onion, shaved

1/4 cup mayonnaise

1 tablespoon sriracha (Thai hot chili sauce)

For the Teriyaki Glaze

1 cup light-brown sugar

1/2 cup sesame oil

1/2 cup soy sauce

3 tablespoons freshly grated ginger

1 tablespoon freshly grated garlic

8 patties Choice ground round, 85% lean, 1/2 pound each, 1 inch thick

Extra virgin olive oil

8 golden hamburger buns, split

Fine sea salt

Directions

To make the slaw, combine the broccoli, cabbage, carrots, bell pepper and onion in a medium bowl. Stir in the mayonnaise and sriracha. Cover and refrigerate.

Prepare the grill for direct cooking at 400° to 500°F.

While the grill is heating, make the Teriyaki Glaze. Whisk together the brown sugar, sesame oil and soy sauce in a medium bowl. Stir in the ginger and garlic. Separate the glaze into two parts and reserve. Two-thirds is for brushing onto the raw beef. The remaining third is for brushing onto the cooked beef.

Recess the centers of the ground round patties (see page 7 for our tips on creating the perfect burger). Brush the patties on both sides with the Teriyaki Glaze. Let the burgers sit, absorbing some of the flavor, for 5 minutes before grilling.

Brush the olive oil onto the sliced sides of the hamburger buns and then sprinkle with salt.

Place the burgers directly over the hottest part of the fire. If you have special requests for temperature, start well-done burgers earlier and medium-rare burgers later. After they hit the grill, spoon or brush a little more teriyaki glaze on the top of the burgers.

For medium burgers, cook for about 12 to 15 minutes total, turning once. When you turn the burgers over, brush or spoon some more glaze on the cooked side (using the glaze that was reserved for cooked beef).

As the burgers near completion, add the buns to the grill, cut-side down. Cook until lightly toasted without drying the buns out. Remove the buns from the grill. Transfer the cooked burgers to the buns. Add a generous spoonful of slaw on top of each burger.

Orange Teriyaki Beef Kebabs

Beef tri-tip (a cut from the bottom sirloin) is tender and perfect for kebabs, and the homemade teriyaki gets a flavor boost from fresh orange for a winning combination.

Serves 6

For the Orange Teriyaki Sauce

3 cups freshly squeezed orange juice

1½ cups light-brown sugar

3/4 cup toasted sesame oil

3/4 cup soy sauce

2 tablespoons freshly grated garlic (use a microplane)

4 tablespoons freshly grated ginger (use a ginger grater or microplane)

For the Kebabs

1½ pounds tri-tip beef, cubed

1 red bell pepper, cut into squares

1 orange bell pepper, cut into squares

1 sweet onion, cut into squares

1/2 pound cubed fresh pineapple

24 large fresh spinach leaves

6 skewers, about 8 inches long (see skewer notes on page 15)

Directions

In a medium saucepan, reduce the 3 cups of orange juice down to 1 cup over medium heat.

For the Orange Teriyaki Sauce, whisk 1 cup of light-brown sugar together with the sesame oil, soy sauce, garlic, ginger and orange juice reduction.

Reserve 1/2 cup of the sauce. Combine the rest with the beef in a zip-top freezer bag. Remove as much air as possible, seal and refrigerate for about 2 hours. Stir the remaining 1/2 cup sugar into the reserved 1/2 cup sauce. Cover and refrigerate to use later for basting.

When it is time to prepare for cooking, get the grill ready for direct grilling at about 400°F.

Assemble the kebabs, alternating between beef, bell peppers, onion, pineapple and folded spinach leaves.

Grill the kebabs over direct heat for a few minutes per side, brushing with the reserved Orange Teriyaki Sauce each time you turn the kebabs. Total cooking time should be about 10 minutes for beef cooked to medium doneness. Be careful not to slop too much sauce onto the grill while you baste, because the sugars will burn quickly.

Serve hot.

Fresh Summer Chili

The fresh summer flavors of tomatoes and corn are delightfully highlighted in this simple chili recipe, which forgoes the heavy flavors of traditional chili seasonings. We use steak with a three-bean blend, but this recipe is also fantastic if you substitute black beans and chicken or even mahi mahi. The key to great chili is great tomatoes. Splurge on very sweet heirloom tomatoes with complex flavors. Pink Brandywine and Cherokee Purple are fantastic choices.

Serves 6

About 4 tablespoons extra virgin olive oil

5 pounds Brandywine or Cherokee Purple tomatoes, cut to a medium dice

6 garlic cloves, finely chopped

1 lime, halved

Fine sea salt

1¼ pounds skirt steak

1 or 2 poblano chiles (depending on whether you would like mild or medium chili)

2 ears corn, shucked

15-ounce can chili bean blend (kidney, pinto and red beans), rinsed and drained

Finely ground white pepper

Variations: For low-fat chicken chili, substitute chicken breasts for the steak and use a 15-ounce can of black beans. Thinly slice the chicken or pound it thin so it grills very quickly and evenly with the same combination of lime, olive oil and salt. Remove the chicken when it is just barely cooked through, as it will continue cooking when you add it to the hot chili.

For an even more creative chili, try using mahi mahi, again grilled with the same combination of lime, olive oil and salt, and again substituting black beans for the chili bean blend.

Directions

Prepare the grill for direct grilling over a medium-high fire (about 500°F). A wood fire is preferred.

Preheat a 12-inch cast iron skillet directly on the grill or over high heat on a side burner. Add 2 tablespoons olive oil to the skillet, then add the tomatoes, garlic, juice of 1/2 lime and 1 teaspoon of fine sea salt. Reduce the tomatoes to a soup consistency while stirring occasionally. This should require 20 to 30 minutes. Other ingredients will be added to the skillet during that time, and the steak will be started as well.

Rinse the skirt steak under cold water and then pat dry with paper towels. Squeeze the remaining 1/2 lime over the steak. Lightly brush with olive oil and sprinkle with sea salt.

Quickly roast the poblano(s) over the hottest part of the grill, turning occasionally, until the skins are blackened and blistered on all sides. Transfer to a paper bag and seal to let the roasted poblano(s) steam for 5 minutes.

Quickly grill the corn over the hottest part of the grill, turning occasionally, until nicely marked on all sides but not fully cooked. Remove from the grill. Once you can handle the corn easily enough, cut the kernels from the cob and reserve.

Scrape the blackened skin from the poblano(s), remove the stem(s) and then cut the flesh into small dice. Add the flesh and seeds to the tomato mixture. Add the corn kernels at this time as well.

About 10 minutes before the tomato mixture will reach its desired texture, it is time to grill the steak. If the tomato mixture is thickening too quickly, move the skillet to a cooler part of the grill or lower the flame on the side burner.

Grill the skirt steak directly over a medium-hot fire to medium-rare doneness, turning once, about 2 to 3 minutes per side. If in doubt, cut into one of the steaks to check doneness. (The steak will quickly cook to medium doneness when it is added to the chili.) Transfer to a cutting board and let rest for a couple of minutes. Cut the steak crosswise into 2-inch sections, cutting with the grain of the meat. Next, thinly slice each of the 2-inch sections, cutting across the grain.

Add the sliced steak, the juice from the cutting board and the beans to the skillet, stirring constantly until the beans are hot. Adjust the flavor as needed with white pepper and sea salt. Serve immediately.

Hearty Winter Chili

To many, chili is the ultimate "man food" and the ultimate expression of culinary independence. This recipe fits the bill on both counts with smoked pork belly and our own Not-So-Basic Barbecue Rub in place of traditional chili powder. Despite the long cooking time, the recipe is not a lot of work. Prepare it a day ahead and reheat it for the game. You will need a 5½- or 7-quart cast iron Dutch oven.

As written, I would call this a medium heat chili. For a more mild chili, cut the chipotle and jalapeño amounts by half.

Serves 10

3 to 4 tablespoons Not-So-Basic Barbecue Rub (see recipe on page 17)

2 pounds pork belly, cut into squares roughly 4 x 4 inches

About 3 cups wood chips, soaked for at least 1 hour (I use maple)

1 tablespoon canola oil

3 to 3½ pounds beef tri-tip, cut into 1/4 inch cubes

12-ounce bottle of brown ale (I use Bell's Best Brown Ale)

2 pounds Roma tomatoes, roughly chopped

1 teaspoon ground cumin

4 chipotle peppers (canned in adobo sauce), finely chopped

2 tablespoons adobo sauce

2 fresh jalapeños, finely chopped

1/2 large red onion, diced

16 ounces frozen corn kernels, thawed

2 cans (15 ounces each) chili bean mix (pinto, kidney and black), rinsed and drained

6 to 12 ounces tomato paste

Sour cream, shredded cheese and sliced green onions for garnish

Directions

Prepare the grill for indirect cooking with wood smoke at 325°F.

Rub 1 to 2 tablespoons Not-So-Basic Barbecue Rub onto both sides of the pork belly pieces. Add the wood chips to the grill, place the pork in the indirect cooking zone and close the hood to begin smoking. I get this going before prepping all the other ingredients. The pork belly can get about an hour of smoking in while you cut up all the other ingredients.

One hour into smoking the pork belly (it will smoke for 4 hours total time), heat a 5½-quart (or larger) cast iron Dutch oven over medium-high heat. Add the canola oil. Brown the tri-tip for a few minutes, working in small batches to avoid over-crowding the pot. Remove and reserve each batch of beef as it is finished. Remove the final batch and deglaze the pot with the beer.

Add the tomatoes to the pot and return to a simmer. Stir in 2 tablespoons Not-So-Basic Barbecue Rub, plus the cumin, chipotles, adobo sauce and jalapeños. Stir in the beef, onion and corn. The beans and tomato paste will not be added until the final hour of cooking.

Place the pot on the grill in the indirect cooking zone without its lid. The lid stays off the pot the entire time the chili is cooking. Close the grill and cook for 4 hours. Keep the wood smoke going the entire time. A skin of smoky goodness will form on top of the chili. Stir this in every 30 minutes or so for maximum flavor.

After the chili has cooked for 3 hours, stir in the beans. Remove the pork belly from the grill, cut it into 1/4 inch cubes and stir it into the chili. If the chili has not thickened most of the way to your desired consistency by this time, stir in 6 to 12 ounces of tomato paste to thicken as needed. (Remember, the chili will thicken as it cools, and it will be thicker the next day, even after re-heating.) Continue cooking for another hour.

Serve the chili with sour cream, grated cheese and sliced green onions on the side.

Skirt Steak Sandwiches with Peaches and Blue Cheese on Grilled Flatbread

Few things can beat the satisfaction, flavor and texture of perfectly grilled homemade flatbread, so these sandwiches are off to a great start. Add to that the delicious combination of skirt steak and roasted peaches, and you have a memorable winner for any summer party.

Serves 8

1 recipe naan (page 161)

8 ounces blue cheese (I use smoked blue cheese)

3 ripe yellow peaches, pitted and diced

2 jalapeños, sliced into very thin rings (discard the seeds if you want to reduce the heat)

2 tablespoons unsalted butter

4 slices red onion, about 1/4 inch thick

Extra virgin olive oil

Kosher salt

2 pounds skirt steak

Directions

Prepare 8 flatbreads using naan recipe.

Prepare the grill for direct and indirect cooking, with the direct zone at about 600°F. Preheat a cast iron skillet in the indirect grilling zone. Add the blue cheese, peaches, jalapeños and butter to the hot skillet and roast until the peaches begin to soften and the blue cheese has melted, but not so long that the jalapeños lose their color. The cooking time should be about 10 to 15 minutes.

Brush the onion slices with olive oil and sprinkle with salt. Grill them over direct heat while the peaches are roasting, about 4 minutes per side. Inserting toothpicks from the sides through the rings will help keep the onion slices together.

Rinse and dry the skirt steak. Brush with olive oil and sprinkle with salt. When the peaches and onions are about ready, put the steak onto the hottest part of the grill. Cook over direct heat, turning once, until cooked to medium. The time will vary with the thickness of the steak but is usually around 4 minutes per side. The secret to great skirt steak is to cook it quickly and to medium doneness. Remove it from the grill, let it rest 2 to 3 minutes, and then slice it thinly across the grain of the meat.

Combine the skirt steak, some red onion and the roasted peach mixture and arrange onto a warm flatbread to serve each sandwich. Then enjoy the accolades from your guests.

Porterhouse Steak with Red Zinfandel Sauce and Portobellos

With a filet on one side of the bone and New York strip on the other, the porterhouse is considered by many to be the king of steaks. A big, beefy porterhouse like this can be prepared beautifully charred on the outside and rare on the inside. The simple Red Zinfandel Sauce is a hearty and sweet marriage of complex flavors. Serving the sauce under the steak allows each person to use as much or as little as they like with each bite.

Generously Serves 2

2-inch-thick porterhouse steak, about 2½ pounds

Extra virgin olive oil

Fine sea salt

1 or 2 portobello mushrooms, sliced thick

1 cup Red Zinfandel Sauce (recipe follows)

Red Zinfandel Sauce

1 750ml bottle of American red zinfandel wine (nearly 3 cups)

1 cup beef broth

1 cup light-brown sugar

1/4 cup soy sauce

Combine the ingredients in a wide pan (the wider the pan, the quicker the reduction) and reduce to about 1 cup, whisking frequently, over medium heat. Keep warm or reheat for serving.

Directions

Prepare the grill for direct grilling over a hot fire (about 500° to 600°F). A wood fire is preferred.

Rinse the steak under cold water and then pat dry with paper towels. Lightly brush with olive oil and sprinkle with sea salt.

Lightly brush the mushroom slices with olive oil and sprinkle with sea salt.

Grill the steak directly over the hot fire, turning once, for 10 minutes or until an instant-read meat thermometer registers 120°F for rare. Remove the steak from the grill and place on a carving board to rest for 5 minutes. During those 5 minutes, grill the mushroom slices over the hot fire for 1 to 2 minutes per side.

Pour the Red Zinfandel Sauce into a preheated platter. Cut the filet section of the steak and strip section away from the bone, then slice each perpendicular to the bone. Reconstruct the slices and bone into the porterhouse shape on top of the sauce in the warm platter. Add the grilled mushroom slices and serve.

Alder-Planked Filet Mixed Grill

Cooking food on a wooden plank imparts a subtle flavor that varies with the species of wood. It also can be a much more forgiving cooking technique than placing food directly over the fire. There are no flare-ups, and the indirect cooking approach slows down all the action.

Serves 4

4 alder wood planks, 5 inches wide x 16 inches long x 3/4 inches thick (see note bottom-right), soaked for at least 4 hours

4 8-ounce beef tenderloin filets

8 slices prosciutto

2 zucchini squashes

2 yellow squashes

2 small red onions

Extra virgin olive oil

Kosher salt or fine sea salt

4 cloves garlic, in the husks

8 sprigs fresh rosemary

Directions

After the planks are soaked, prepare a grill for indirect grilling at 400° to 500°F.

Wrap the perimeter of each steak with 2 slices of prosciutto and hold in place with toothpicks. Set aside at room temperature while you prepare the vegetables.

Slice the zucchini and yellow squash lengthwise in quarters after trimming off the ends. Cut the quarters into pieces about 3/4 inch long, keeping the sizes as consistent as possible. Transfer to a medium bowl. Slice the onions into eighths with each wedge ending with a little bit of the root base to hold all the layers together. Peel off the outer layer from each edge and discard. Add the onion wedges to the bowl. Gently toss the veggies in the bowl with a little olive oil to coat.

Brush both sides of the filets with olive oil and season with salt. Place one filet on each board. Distribute the veggies evenly on the boards. Add a clove of garlic, still in its husk, to each board. Add one sprig of rosemary near each steak (you'll use the other sprigs later). Sprinkle salt over all the veggies.

Place the boards in the indirect cooking zone (the area without fire below) directly on the grill grate. Close the hood and roast for about 30 minutes or until an instant read thermometer registers 115°F inside the meat. Turn the steaks over at the halfway point. Once they read 115°F, remove the steaks from the boards and put them in the direct zone above the fire. If you are using a gas grill, crank up the heat under the steaks. If you are using a charcoal grill, open up the air vents all the way. Grill for about 2 minutes per side to get slight grill marks. Return the steaks to the boards and remove the boards from the grill. Remove and discard the exhausted rosemary sprigs. Replace with fresh ones for serving.

You can serve the mixed grills right on the planks. I suggest putting each plank on a platter if you can. Let the steaks rest for 5 minutes before digging in.

Note: You can purchase pre-packaged alder planks at better food markets or cooking stores, but I find it more economical to go to a hardwood specialty store where you can buy furniture-grade hardwood. There, you can have the staff cut the species of wood you like to the sizes you like. You can also get the thicker boards like I recommend using here. The planks are reusable for at least a few cooking sessions. Simply wash them off after each use and be sure you keep them in the indirect cooking zone so they don't catch on fire.

Ribeye Steak with Gorgonzola-Jalapeño Butter

A big old bone-in ribeye is positively majestic on its own. The addition of Gorgonzola-Jalapeño Butter kicks up the flavor a notch or two.

Serves 2

2 bone-in ribeye steaks, about 1½ inches thick

Extra virgin olive oil

Kosher salt

For the Gorgonzola-Jalapeño Butter

2 tablespoons unsalted butter, at room temperature

1/4 cup crumbled Gorgonzola cheese

Zest of 1/2 lemon

As many rings of thinly sliced jalapeño peppers as desired

Directions

Prepare the grill for direct grilling at about 500°F. A wood fire is preferred.

Rinse and dry the steaks. Brush them all over with olive oil and sprinkle with salt.

Combine the butter, cheese, lemon zest and jalapeño in a small bowl. Reserve.

Grill the steaks in the direct cooking zone to the desired doneness, turning once. A few minutes before removing the steaks from the grill, top each with the reserved Gorgonzola-Jalapeño Butter.

For medium-rare, this ribeye steak grilled at 500°F should require about 15 minutes total cooking time.

Steak with Fire-Roasted Tomatoes, Olives and Pistachios

Our combination of roasted ingredients complements a perfectly grilled steak without masking its flavor. I used two kinds of heirloom tomatoes here, chosen for their slightly tart taste, but quality hothouse tomatoes also will do the trick. The pistachios become tender when roasted in the pan along with the other ingredients.

Serves 2

2 New York strip steaks, at least 1¼ inches thick

About 2 tablespoons extra virgin olive oil

Fine sea salt

5 Spanish "queen" olives in brine

1 pound ripe, medium-size tomatoes

1 heaping tablespoon shelled pistachios

1 large clove garlic, minced

1/2 teaspoon coarse sea salt

1 teaspoon balsamic vinegar

Directions

Prepare the grill for direct grilling over a medium-high fire (500° to 600°F) with an indirect cooking zone as well. A wood fire is preferred. For grilling with wood chunks, reserve 1 wood chunk to add to a corner of the fire right before you start grilling. This chunk will provide smoke and an open flame to enhance the flavor. The steaks can be cooked near, but not over, the flaming wood chunk.

Preheat a 10-inch cast iron skillet in the direct grilling zone with the grill hood closed.

Remove the steaks from the refrigerator 20 minutes prior to grilling. Rinse them and dry with paper towels. Brush with 1 tablespoon of the olive oil and sprinkle with fine sea salt.

Remove the olives from the brine and dry with paper towels to remove some of the moisture. Pit and sliver or finely chop.

Cut the tomatoes into quarters lengthwise and remove the stems. Slice the quarters crosswise to 3/8 inch thick.

When ready to grill, move the skillet to the indirect cooking zone. Add 1 tablespoon of olive oil to the skillet, immediately followed by the tomatoes, olives, pistachios and garlic. Add the coarse sea salt and balsamic vinegar, then stir gently to combine.

Place the steaks in the direct grilling zone. For medium-rare, cook the steaks for about 10 to 12 minutes, turning only once. Keep the hood closed to roast the tomatoes, olives and pistachios while you grill the steak. Gently stir the mixture when you turn the steaks, being careful not to break up the tomatoes too much.

When nearing the desired doneness (see Food Temperature Chart on page 162), remove the steaks from the grill and let rest a few minutes before serving. While resting, top the steaks with the tomato, olive and pistachio mixture.

Pasture-Raised Veal Chops with Herbed Cheese Butter and Fried Sage

The herbed cheese butter in this dish is outstanding with the veal chop or as a steak topper. It also is a nice complement to lobster if you're in the mood for surf and turf. The fried sage leaves are a quick and easy way to dress up a perfectly grilled dish. I recommend grilling the chops directly over a wood fire for the best flavor.

Serves 2

2 pasture-raised veal rib chops, about 2/3 pound each

Extra virgin olive oil

Fine sea salt

For the Herbed Cheese Butter

2 tablespoons unsalted butter, at room temperature

2 tablespoons Boursin soft garlic and herb cheese

1/2 teaspoon freshly grated lemon zest

1/2 teaspoon coarse sea salt

For the Fried Sage

Canola oil

4 fresh sage leaves, rinsed and thoroughly dried

Directions

Prepare the grill for direct cooking at 400° to 500°F.

Rinse and dry the chops. Brush them all over with olive oil and sprinkle on both sides with fine sea salt. Let the chops rise to room temperature while you are getting the fire ready, about 20 minutes.

Thoroughly combine the butter, cheese, lemon zest and coarse sea salt in a small bowl. Use the backside of a spoon to blend the butter and cheese together against the sides of the bowl.

Also while the grill is getting ready, heat an 8-inch frying pan over medium heat. Once heated, add 1/8 inch canola oil to the pan. Once the surface of the oil begins to wrinkle, add the 4 sage leaves. Fry the leaves until they are crisp and deep green in color. If they begin to brown, they have been fried too long. I find it best to use chopsticks for moving the leaves around and removing them from the oil. You also can pick them up to see when they are crisp and ready to remove. Transfer the fried leaves to a paper towel until serving.

Grill the chops over direct heat, about 6 minutes per side for medium (140° to 150°F internal temperature). About 2 minutes before they are done, top each chop with a third of the butter/cheese mixture and close the grill hood to melt. Check after 1 minute. If too much of the topping has run off, you can add more from the remaining third. Transfer the chops to a pair of preheated plates and top each with 2 fried sage leaves.

Beer-Braised Short Ribs with Roasted Cauliflower and Pumpkin Seeds

There are two keys to great short ribs: One, braise them slowly until the meat is so tender it nearly falls off the bone; and two, crisp them quickly over a direct fire right before serving. Pairing them with hearty accompaniments is also a must. This recipe gives you simple instructions for achieving the perfect short ribs, braised in Belgian ale, and we can guarantee the accompaniments will be a hit. Roasted cauliflower, fingerling potatoes and cherry tomatoes are lightly caramelized and flavored by apple wood smoke. Roasted pumpkin seeds add a special crunch.

Serves 6

For the Short Ribs

6 beef short ribs, about 6 pounds total

Kosher salt

Olive oil

2 to 3 cups Belgian ale

12- to 14-inch covered cast iron skillet or large Dutch oven

For the Roasted Vegetables

1 large head of fresh cauliflower, broken down into bite-sized pieces

1 pound red fingerling potatoes, halved lengthwise

8 cloves garlic, sliced

1½ pounds multi-colored cherry tomato medley or grape tomatoes

Extra virgin olive oil

Kosher salt

1 cup apple wood chips, soaked

1/4 cup raw pumpkin seeds

12- to 14-inch cast iron skillet

8- to 10-inch cast iron skillet

Directions

Prepare the grill for indirect cooking at 400°F. Preheat a cast iron skillet or Dutch oven directly over the fire. The total cooking time will be about 3 hours with wood smoke added for the final hour.

Liberally salt the short ribs. Add a small amount of oil to the preheated skillet. With the skillet directly over the fire, brown the ribs for about 3 minutes per side. Avoid overcrowding the skillet. Brown the ribs in 2 batches if necessary.

Place all of the ribs in the skillet, add the Belgian ale, cover and position the skillet in the indirect cooking zone. Cook for 1 hour with the hood closed, then turn the ribs over and rotate the skillet 180 degrees. Cover and continue indirect cooking for another hour. At the 2-hour point, turn the ribs and the skillet again and add the vegetables to the grill (details follow).

About 1 hour and 50 minutes into cooking the beef, add 2 more skillets to the grill to preheat. Combine the cauliflower, potatoes and garlic in a large bowl along with about 1/2 cup olive oil and 1 teaspoon salt. Toss to coat. Combine the tomatoes with a little salt and olive oil in a separate bowl. At the 2-hour point, add the tomatoes to the smaller skillet and the cauliflower mixture to the other skillet. Both should remain uncovered, placed in the indirect cooking zone. Start the apple wood smoke, close the grill, and cook the vegetables alongside the ribs for about 45 minutes, turning the cauliflower mixture once.

At the 2 hour and 45 minute mark, transfer the tomatoes into the skillet with the cauliflower mixture. Wipe down the smaller skillet to prepare it for toasting the pumpkin seeds. Close the grill and continue roasting for 15 more minutes. The cauliflower and potatoes should be browned around the edges and starting to turn crisp.

During the final 15 minutes of grilling, toast the pumpkin seeds in the small skillet over a cooktop burner at medium heat, tossing constantly until brown and popping. Drain on paper towels.

At the 3 hour mark, transfer the braised ribs from the skillet onto the grill grate in the direct grilling zone. They will be very tender at this point, so treat them gently. Crisp up the outside of the ribs over the fire for a few minutes and then transfer them to a serving platter. Transfer the roasted vegetables to a serving bowl and toss them with the roasted pumpkin seeds. Serve alongside the ribs.

Horseradish-Crusted Rib Roast

A rib roast creates a sense of occasion like no other cut. I prefer to cook it on the grill, adding flavor from a little smoke. Our horseradish crust is easy to prepare and builds a crunchy and flavorful layer on the outer edge of the roast. Serve the roast plain or with your favorite horseradish sauce on the side.

Serves 8 to 10

1/3 cup horseradish, finely grated

2 tablespoons prepared Dijon mustard

7 large cloves garlic, crushed

2 tablespoons fresh rosemary, chopped

1 tablespoon fresh thyme, chopped

Finely grated zest of 2 lemons

2 teaspoons coarse sea salt

1 teaspoon coarse black pepper

1 tablespoon extra virgin olive oil

1 bone-in rib roast, about 6 pounds

2 cups of your favorite wood chips (I like to use apple, and I sneak a few rosemary sprigs into the smoking envelope with the wood), soaked

Directions

Prepare the grill for indirect grilling at about 350°F.

Thoroughly combine all ingredients except the roast and the wood chips in a bowl. Dry off the roast and place bone-side down on a board or other prep surface. Coat the top of the roast with the horseradish paste and let sit at room temperature for about 20 minutes.

Place the roast directly on the grill grate with the bone-side down in the indirect cooking zone. Add the wood chips as appropriate for your grill (see page 5).

Cook over indirect heat with the grill closed for 1½ to 2 hours, or until the internal temperature reads 125°F for medium-rare and the horseradish crust has browned and become crisp. (You can control the degree of browning of the crust by the proximity of the roast to the fire, but keep the roast in the indirect zone at all times.) Remove from the grill and let rest for 10 minutes. The internal temperature should continue to rise to medium-rare.

Carve and serve on a warm platter.

Smoke-Roasted Rack of Lamb with Savory Rosemary Rub

Alder wood smoke lends its subtle support to this recipe, highlighting the tenderness of perfectly cooked lamb and the flavors of rosemary and garlic.

Serves 4

2 racks of lamb, frenched, 2 to 2½ pounds total

Extra virgin olive oil

1 batch Savory Rosemary Rub (recipe follows)

Aluminum foil

2 cups alder wood chips, soaked

Savory Rosemary Rub

6 large cloves garlic, minced

4 tablespoons fresh rosemary, finely chopped

Finely grated zest from 2 lemons

3 teaspoons coarse sea salt

3 teaspoons coarsely ground black pepper

Combine all ingredients. Refrigerate for up to 4 hours before use.

Directions

Prepare the grill for indirect cooking at 350° to 375°F.

Let the lamb racks rest and come up to room temperature for about 15 minutes.

Brush the lamb on all sides with olive oil. Press the Savory Rosemary Rub onto all sides except the two ends of each rack.

Wrap the exposed bones with aluminum foil to prevent them from burning and becoming brittle. Place the lamb racks in the indirect cooking zone with the bone-side down and the bones pointed away from the heat source. Add the alder wood chips for smoke (learn about smoking techniques on page 5 or at *KalamazooGourmet.com*) and roast with the hood closed until an instant-read thermometer measures 135° to 140°F, about 30 to 40 minutes.

Remove the lamb from the grill and let it rest for about 2 minutes before slicing. Slice the racks into chops and serve on a preheated platter.

Quick and Aromatic Barbecue Ribs

The best way to cook tender ribs is "low and slow." The traditional smoking method is done at about 225°F for many hours, but it can be difficult to find that much time on a busy weekend. This recipe uses a cherry juice and beer "sauna" to accelerate the cooking process as much as possible without sacrificing the tenderness. The intense, distinctive flavors of cherry, cinnamon and allspice will prove to be quite a hit.

Serves 6

3 cups cherry wood chips

3 slabs St. Louis-style ribs (baby-back ribs will work) with the membrane removed

1 batch Not-So-Basic Barbecue Rub (see recipe on page 17)

Aluminum foil

1 cup beer (Hacker-Pschorr Weiss is a good flavor choice)

1 cup unsweetened (tart) cherry juice

Foil turkey roasting pan

1 cup honey

For the Barbecue Finishing Sauce

1 cup ketchup

1 cup honey

2 tablespoons light-brown sugar

3 tablespoons apple-cider vinegar

2 teaspoons Tabasco hot sauce

1 teaspoon freshly ground black pepper

1 teaspoon chili powder

1/2 teaspoon Colman's mustard powder

1/2 teaspoon ground cumin

1/4 teaspoon ground cinnamon

1/2 teaspoon ground allspice

Directions

Soak 2 cups of the cherry wood chips in water for about an hour.

Prepare your grill for indirect cooking at 325°F.

Rinse the ribs under cool water and pat dry with paper towels. Cut each rack into 2 half-racks (or have the butcher do it for you). If the butcher did not remove the silvery membranes from the "bone side" of the racks for you, remove them now.

Rub the "bone side" of the racks with about a quarter of the Not-So-Basic Barbecue Rub. Rub the remainder into the "meat side" and let rest for about 20 minutes.

About 15 minutes before you put the ribs on the grill, create 2 foil smoking envelopes (see instructions on page 5) and put 1 on the grill to get started.

Add the ribs to the grill with the "meat side" up in the indirect cooking zone. If your grill is too small for all the racks to lay flat, use a rib rack to hold them on end. Cover the grill and cook for about 90 minutes at 325°F. Add the second smoking envelope after the first 30 minutes.

Place the beer and cherry juice in the foil roasting pan. Remove the ribs from the grill. Baste both sides of the racks with honey and place in the pan with the "meat side" up. Overlap the racks a little if necessary to make them fit or use a rib rack. Cover with foil and return to the indirect zone of the grill.

Cook with the grill closed for 60 minutes more, or until tender and cooked through. Test to see that the meat pierces easily with a toothpick. Cook longer if necessary, adding more cherry juice if the liquid runs low.

During this period, prepare the Barbecue Finishing Sauce. Combine all the ingredients in a pot. Stir over medium heat until simmering and thoroughly combined. Remove from heat.

Transfer the racks from the foil pan onto the direct grilling zone. Baste with warm Barbecue Finishing Sauce and cook for about 2 minutes per side. Baste with a little more sauce and repeat, then serve.

Note: This recipe is great for bringing to barbecues away from home. Cook the ribs in advance up to the point where they should come out of the foil pan. Wrap the racks tightly in foil and refrigerate until it is almost time to serve. Borrow your host's grill for a few minutes to reheat the ribs and baste with the Barbecue Finishing Sauce as described above, but do it for a little longer to allow the ribs to reheat.

Brat Burgers with Fennel Mustard Seed Slaw

One of the best parts of cooking from scratch is that you know exactly what is in the food you eat. This has never been truer than with sausage. While it's a great food, there are often questions as to what is actually in there. These brat burgers are made from pork shoulder and delicately spiced with juniper berries and fragrant cardamom pods. The fennel slaw on top will make your mouth water.

If you are new to making sausage, this recipe is a great one to start with because you don't need to fuss with any casings. If you prefer not to grind your own pork, you can mix the spices in this recipe into 80% lean pre-ground pork.

Serves 6

For the Brat Burgers

3 pounds pork shoulder

1 teaspoon kosher salt

1/2 teaspoon ground Aleppo chile (you can find this at Williams Sonoma)

1/2 teaspoon freshly ground coriander

1/2 teaspoon freshly ground cardamom

1/2 teaspoon freshly ground juniper berries

For the Fennel Mustard Seed Slaw

1/4 cup mayonnaise

1 teaspoon whole black mustard seed, coarsely ground

1/2 teaspoon champagne vinegar

2 pinches fine sea salt

About 6 ounces of thinly shaved fennel bulb plus the wispy fronds

6 slices Emmenthaler Swiss cheese

6 pretzel hamburger buns, sliced

6 large tomato slices

Directions

Cut the pork shoulder into 1/2-inch cubes. Pork shoulder is roughly 80% lean, so it is perfect for a grilled burger application like this. Place the meat pieces in a single layer and sprinkle evenly with the salt, Aleppo chile, coriander, cardamom and juniper berries. Please note that the flavor of freshly ground spices is much stronger than pre-ground spices. A coffee grinder is a perfect piece of equipment for the task. Transfer the seasoned meat to a metal bowl, cover and refrigerate for 1 to 2 hours. A metal bowl will help transfer the cold to the meat. It is important that the fat be well-chilled prior to grinding.

Prepare the Fennel Mustard Seed Slaw. Place the mayonnaise, mustard seed, champagne vinegar and salt in a medium mixing bowl. Whisk to thoroughly combine. Toss in the fennel and reserve.

Use a meat grinder, a food grinder attachment on your mixer or a food processor to finely grind the meat. Form into 6 equal patties, slightly larger than the buns and recessed in the middles. (See page 7 for our tips on creating the perfect burger.)

Prepare the grill for direct grilling over a medium-hot fire, about 500°F. Grill the burgers, turning once, until cooked through, about 5 minutes per side. Add a slice of cheese to each for the last minute of cooking. Lightly toast the buns on the grill at this time.

Assemble the burgers with a slice of tomato and some Fennel Mustard Seed Slaw and serve.

Roasted Pork Chops with Blueberries and Pancetta

Pork and fruit are well-matched, especially pork and blueberries. These glorious chops blend smoky, sweet and savory flavors.

Serves 4

4 pork loin chops, preferably bone-in, about 1½ inches thick

Extra virgin olive oil

1/2 teaspoon smoked salt, plus salt for the chops

1/2 cup pure maple syrup

1 pint blueberries

6 ounces pancetta (rolled Italian bacon), cooked crisp and broken up

Directions

Preheat the grill for combination direct cooking and indirect cooking. The indirect zone should be at about 500°F.

While the grill is heating, rinse and dry the chops. Lightly brush them on all sides with olive oil and sprinkle with salt. Smoked salt will jump-start the smoky flavor and is good to use for this recipe even when grilling over a wood fire. Leave the chops sitting at room temperature while the grill is getting ready, up to 20 minutes. Wash the blueberries at this time.

Grill the pork chops over direct heat for about 2 minutes per side and then transfer them to the indirect cooking zone. Close the grill and cook the chops for about 20 minutes, turning once halfway through, until an instant-read meat thermometer measures 155°F when inserted away from the bone.

As soon as you have moved the chops to the indirect zone, combine the maple syrup, blueberries and 1/2 teaspoon smoked salt in a large saucepan (although the ingredients would easily fit in a smaller pan, the broader bottom should help reduce the sauce more quickly) and bring to a strong simmer over medium heat. Stir the sauce frequently and avoid a rapid boil. If bubbles begin to build on top of bubbles, lower the heat to avoid burning the sauce.

When cooked to 155°F internal temperature, remove the chops from the grill and transfer to plates. Let the chops rest 3 to 5 minutes. During this time, stir the cooked pancetta into the blueberry sauce. Top the chops with the sauce, serve and enjoy.

Crown Roast of Pork with Savory Rosemary Rub

The majesty of a crown roast belies the simplicity of its preparation — especially if the butcher ties it for you.

Complementing the pork is a Savory Rosemary Rub (the same rub used on the lamb on page 57). Fresh rosemary, garlic and lemon zest combine with salt and pepper to create a delicious crust outside the roast.

Serves about 8

Crown pork roast, tied, about 6 pounds (approximately 12 ribs)

Extra virgin olive oil

1 batch Savory Rosemary Rub (recipe follows)

Hickory wood chunks or soaked chips

Chicken or beef stock (optional)

Aluminum foil (optional)

Savory Rosemary Rub

6 large cloves garlic, minced

4 tablespoons fresh rosemary, finely chopped

Finely grated zest from 2 lemons

3 teaspoons coarse sea salt

3 teaspoons coarsely ground black pepper

Combine all ingredients. Refrigerate for up to 4 hours before use.

Directions

Brush the pork roast all over with olive oil and then press the Savory Rosemary Rub into the roast, avoiding the bones. Allow the roast to rise toward room temperature for about 30 minutes before putting it on the grill.

Prepare a grill for indirect cooking at about 400°F. For hybrid grills, light a wood fire on one half of the grill and let it burn just until the wood is covered with gray ash and very hot. For gas grills, prepare to use wet wood chips for smoking.

If you plan to make gravy for the roast or the dressing, a roasting pan and rack will be needed. For something as small as this pork roast, I like to place a wire rack across the top of a 12-inch cast iron skillet, cooking the roast on the rack. If using a roasting pan, place 1/2 inch to 1 inch of stock in the bottom of the pan. If not, the roast can be cooked directly on the grill grate. Either way, place the roast in the indirect cooking zone, close the hood and cook at 400°F for 2 to 2½ hours or until the internal temperature measures 150°F. Rotate the roast a few times along the way to ensure even cooking, but keep the hood closed as much as possible. If the bones begin to char, cover them with foil.

Remove from the grill, loosely cover with foil and let the roast rest for 15 to 20 minutes before serving. Gravy can be prepared during this resting period.

Barbecued Shrimp Skewers with Peach Salsa

The spiced rub on the shrimp is balanced by sweet peach salsa in this fantastic summer appetizer.

Serves 8 as an Appetizer

For the Peach Salsa

1/2 lime

3 ripe yellow peaches

1/4 red onion, sliced very thin

1/4 red bell pepper, diced

2 tablespoons fresh cilantro leaves, chopped

1 jalapeño, seeded and finely chopped

Sugar (optional)

For the Barbecued Shrimp

16 bamboo skewers (or 8 if they are double-pronged like in the photo)

32 shrimp (10 to 15 per pound size), peeled and deveined, tails left on

1 tablespoon Not-So-Basic Barbecue Rub (see recipe on page 17)

2 tablespoons light-brown sugar

For Serving

8 lime wedges

Directions

To make 3 cups of peach salsa: Juice the 1/2 lime into a medium-sized bowl. Dice the peaches and immediately stir into the lime juice. Add the onion, red pepper and cilantro. Stir in 1/2 of the jalapeño and test the salsa for heat. Add as much of the remaining jalapeño as appropriate for your taste or the tastes of your guests. If the peaches were not ripe enough or otherwise did not deliver enough sweetness, add a small amount of sugar as desired. Cover and refrigerate until ready to serve, up to 4 hours.

Prepare the grill for direct grilling over medium-high heat (about 400°F).

Use double-pronged skewers (like the one in the photo at left) or pairs of skewers to prevent the shrimp from turning. Build 8 double-pronged skewers with 4 shrimp each.

Combine the Not-So-Basic Barbecue Rub with the brown sugar and sprinkle over both sides of the shrimp skewers.

Grill the shrimp over medium-high heat for about 6 minutes, turning once. The shrimp are fully cooked when they become opaque. Try not to overcook the shrimp, or they can become tough.

Serve the shrimp (on or off the skewers) with the peach salsa and lime wedges.

Buffalo Shrimp with Blue Cheese

Swapping tender shrimp for the classic chicken wings is not only a refreshing change of pace, but they can be a little easier to eat as well. You'll still need to discard the tails, but that is much less of a mess than working through all those wing bones.

Serves 4 to 6 as an Appetizer

For the Buffalo Shrimp

1/4 cup Cholula hot sauce, plus extra for drizzling

1/4 cup extra virgin olive oil

1/4 cup freshly squeezed lemon juice

4 garlic cloves, crushed

4½ teaspoons soy sauce

1/2 teaspoon ground coriander

20 shrimp (10 to 15 per pound size), peeled and deveined, tails left on

20 short bamboo skewers, soaked in water for 2 hours

About 1 cup panko (crispy bread crumbs)

For the Blue Cheese Dip

3/4 cup mayonnaise

1/4 cup sour cream

1/2 teaspoon ground black pepper

1 teaspoon finely grated fresh lemon zest

3/4 cup crumbled blue cheese or Gorgonzola

Buttermilk to thin, if necessary

Directions

Whisk together the first 6 ingredients in a large glass or stainless steel bowl to create the marinade. Stir in the shrimp, cover and refrigerate for 4 to 5 hours.

Combine all the blue cheese dip ingredients except the buttermilk in a bowl. As a dip, you may want it pretty thick. To use as a dressing, dilute with buttermilk and stir to reach the desired consistency. Cover and refrigerate for at least 1 hour before use. Note: This buffalo shrimp recipe will only need a half-batch of this dip.

Prepare the grill for direct cooking at 400° to 500°F.

Remove the shrimp from the marinade. Thread each shrimp onto a short skewer so that it will remain straight and can be grilled on all sides. Place the panko on a plate and roll the shrimp skewers in the crumbs to coat one by one. Drizzle the breaded shrimp with a little more Cholula hot sauce.

Grill the shrimp skewers over direct heat, turning occasionally, until cooked through and still tender, about 6 to 8 minutes total. Remove from the grill and serve with Blue Cheese Dip.

Shrimp and Peach Kebabs with Habañero Honey Glaze

Peaches and habañeros are one of my favorite food combinations, whether it is for hot wings, salsa or these kebabs. This recipe is delicious and a snap to make. The glaze also works well for chicken breasts or hot wings.

Serves 6 as an Appetizer

For the Habañero Honey Glaze

3/4 cup honey

3 tablespoons fresh lime juice

2 to 4 habañero chiles, halved

For the Kebabs

About 6 thick slices of bacon

18 shrimp, peeled (the bigger, the better)

2 fresh peaches, pitted and sliced thick

6 flat skewers, about 8 inches long

Directions

Prepare the grill for direct grilling at about 500°F.

Combine the honey and lime juice in a small, nonstick pan and warm up to a very low simmer over low heat. Slice 2 to 4 habañero chiles in half and place in the honey mixture. (Use 2 chiles for a mild version of the dish, more for added fire.) Let the chiles simmer in the honey while you prepare the kebabs. Be careful not to boil the honey.

Cut the bacon slices crosswise into square pieces. Skewer the shrimp, peach slices and bacon pieces, using a piece of bacon between each shrimp and peach slice.

Remove and discard the habañeros from the honey. Grill the shrimp kebabs over direct heat for about 4 minutes per side, until the shrimp and bacon are cooked through. Baste occasionally with the Habañero Honey Glaze along the way. Serve hot.

Lobster Tails with Sweet Ginger Butter

Boiled or steamed lobster breaks my heart. Sweet lobster meat takes on a more complex character when kissed by the heat of an open fire. Rather than the traditional dip in clarified butter, a ginger butter topping makes these lobster tails divine. The compound butter also works very well topping New York strip if you're in the mood for a little surf and turf.

Serves 4

8 fresh or thawed small lobster tails

Extra virgin olive oil

1 lemon

Fine sea salt

1 batch Sweet Ginger Butter (recipe follows)

Sweet Ginger Butter

4 tablespoons unsalted butter, at room temperature

1 tablespoon freshly grated ginger

1 clove garlic, crushed

1 tablespoon plus 2 teaspoons light-brown sugar

1 teaspoon medium-coarse red Hawaiian sea salt (or other high-quality sea salt)

Work the ingredients together in a small bowl until thoroughly combined and relatively smooth. Reserve at room temperature for up to 1 hour.

Directions

Prepare the grill for direct grilling at medium-high heat between 400° and 500°F.

Split the lobster tails in half lengthwise by first cutting the top and bottom shells with scissors and then splitting the flesh with a chef's knife. Lightly brush the flesh sides with olive oil and squeeze some lemon juice over the top. Season with a little fine sea salt.

Grill the lobster for about 5 minutes, turning once. Start with the cut side on the grill and finish with the shell side on the grill. Cook until just opaque.

Remove the lobster from the grill and top with Sweet Ginger Butter. If you like, quickly melt half the ginger butter in the microwave before plating and drizzle this over the top.

Blackened Sea Scallops with Lemon Mustard Stinger Sauce

The aromatic blackening spice blend used here features fennel, coriander and green peppercorns, so these scallops will sing with flavor. The intensity of the mustard in the stinger sauce may remind you of wasabi, so a little dab will do. The blackening spice blend also works well with steak or chicken.

Serves 4 to 6 as an Appetizer

12 large sea scallops, about 1 pound

For the Aromatic Blackening Spice Rub

1 teaspoon whole green peppercorns

1/2 teaspoon whole black peppercorns

1/2 teaspoon whole fennel seeds

1/2 teaspoon whole mustard seeds

1/2 teaspoon whole coriander

1 teaspoon ground cayenne pepper

1 teaspoon smoked paprika

1 teaspoon granulated garlic

1/2 teaspoon coarse sea salt

1/4 teaspoon dried lemon zest

For the Lemon Mustard Stinger Sauce

1 teaspoon Colman's mustard powder

1/2 teaspoon water

1/2 teaspoon soy sauce

1 teaspoon Dijon mustard

2 tablespoons lemon curd (found with the jellies and jams at the supermarket)

Directions

Prepare the grill for direct cooking at 500°F.

Rinse and thoroughly dry the scallops. Let them rise to room temperature, about 10 minutes.

To make the blackening rub, combine the ingredients in a spinning-blade-style coffee grinder or in a mini food processor. Grind until the ingredients are well combined but not too processed.

Combine the mustard powder and water in a small dish and mix together thoroughly. Stir in the soy sauce, Dijon mustard and lemon curd. Transfer to a serving dish.

Dry the scallops one more time. Spread the blackening spice rub on a plate. Press the flat sides of each scallop gently into the spice rub, keeping the sides as free of spices as possible. There is no need to pick up a large amount of the blackening spice on the scallops because the flavor is quite intense.

Grill the scallops over direct heat, turning once, for about 6 minutes per side. Remove from the grill and serve with the sauce on the side.

Grilled Baby Octopus with Cilantro Oil

Perhaps it takes a little bravery, but fresh baby octopus seared over a hot fire is a simple and perfect appetizer. Choose small octopus — the smaller the better — and keep them on ice right up to grilling time. Quick cooking over a hot fire is the secret to tender octopus.

Serves 4

4 baby octopus, less than 1 pound total

Extra virgin olive oil

Kosher salt

Cilantro Oil (recipe follows)

Cilantro Oil
Yields 1 cup

4 ounces cilantro leaves and thinner stem portions, washed and dried

1/3 cup extra virgin olive oil

1/2 teaspoon kosher salt

1 to 2 large cloves garlic, sliced

Combine the cilantro, olive oil, salt and 1 clove of garlic in a blender or food processor. Puree until smooth and thick. Test for taste and add the additional garlic if desired. Extra Cilantro Oil will keep for a few days tightly covered in the refrigerator.

Directions

Prepare the grill for direct cooking at 700° to 800°F. A charcoal fire is preferred.

Prepare the octopus by first removing the beaks. These are the only part you cannot eat. The hoods can be left on or discarded. If the octopus are on the larger side, I discard the hoods.

Lightly coat the octopus with olive oil and season liberally with salt.

Grill the octopus for about 90 seconds per side. Press the octopus into the hot grill surface for better searing. You should hear a high-pitched, soft squeal if the flesh is being seared properly.

Remove from the grill and slice the octopus into individual legs. If serving the hoods, slice those into rings. Serve with the Cilantro Oil while the octopus is still hot from the fire.

The Cilantro Oil is featured on the cover with a grilled ribeye steak. It is a fantastic accompaniment to beef as well as other seafood.

Halibut with Cebollitas and Romesco Sauce

Romesco is a traditional Catalan sauce made with tomatoes, peppers, bread and almonds, and it is a perfect match for grilled meat and fish. Our recipe emphasizes this relationship by grill-roasting the tomatoes, garlic and bread.

Serves 4

For the Romesco Sauce
Yields 2 cups

1/2 cup plus 1 tablespoon extra virgin olive oil

1 to 2 dried pasilla chiles, halved, stemmed and seeded

Water

1/2 cup blanched slivered almonds

6 Roma tomatoes, cored

4 large cloves of garlic in their papery skins

1 to 2 slices country bread

2 tablespoons red-wine vinegar

1/2 teaspoon salt

1/2 teaspoon smoked paprika

For the Halibut and Onions

2 pounds fresh halibut fillets, skin-on, divided into 4 pieces

Extra virgin olive oil

Fine sea salt

12 cebollitas (green onions with larger bulbs than standard green onions — find them at a Hispanic produce market)

Cast iron skillets

Directions

Prepare the grill for indirect and direct grilling with the indirect zone at 450° to 500°F. Preheat 2 cast iron skillets in the indirect zone.

Heat 1 tablespoon olive oil in a medium frying pan over medium heat. Once the surface of the oil begins to wrinkle, add the chiles. Press them into the pan, turning occasionally, until they begin to smoke. Remove the pan from the heat and transfer the chiles to a bowl of water. Use a plate to keep the chiles submerged.

Return the pan to the heat and toast the almonds in the same oil. Reserve.

While the chiles are rehydrating, place the tomatoes and garlic in separate skillets in the indirect cooking zone. Grill the bread slices in the direct zone until marked. Transfer them to the indirect zone and close the hood. Roast the tomatoes and garlic for 10 minutes. Check on the bread after 5 minutes and remove it early if it is becoming overly dry or looks likely to burn.

Remove the skins from the tomato and garlic and discard. Combine the tomatoes, garlic, vinegar, salt, paprika and almonds in a blender or food processor. Cut up the chiles and bread and add half of each to the mix. Start the blender to combine the ingredients then drizzle in the olive oil. Puree until smooth. Test for taste, adding more chile or salt as desired. The sauce can be thickened by adding more of the bread. The finished Romesco Sauce will remain hot until the fish and cebollitas are done.

Prepare the fish by rinsing and drying with paper towels. Brush with olive oil and season with salt.

Rinse and dry the cebollitas.

Place the fish in the direct grilling zone with the skin-side up. The hot grates should release the fish within 2 minutes. Turn 90° for cross-hatch grill marks and continue grilling for 2 more minutes. Flip the fish over to grill the skin side and add the cebollitas to the direct grilling zone. Grill the fish for another 4 minutes or until the flesh begins to flake apart. Turn the cebollitas frequently until well-marked on all sides. If the fish is not flaky after 8 minutes over direct heat, move the fillets to the indirect grilling zone and finish them with the hood closed.

Serve the grilled halibut and cebollitas with the warm Romesco Sauce. Extra Romesco Sauce will keep in the refrigerator for about a week.

Swordfish with Italian Summer Salsa

Salmon may be more forgiving on the grill, but the rewards of a perfectly grilled swordfish steak are unrivaled. I recommend selecting steaks from the belly of the fish, identifiable by the white skin, rather than the back meat which shows a black skin. The best flavors of swordfish are enhanced by a stunning blend of avocado, heirloom tomato, basil and a bit of mozzarella cheese for a perfect summer treat. Any extra Italian summer salsa you make will quickly disappear.

Serves 6

2 heirloom tomatoes

2 tablespoons lemon juice

1/3 cup extra virgin olive oil

2 avocados

3 cloves garlic, thinly sliced

3 ounces goat's milk mozzarella cheese, diced

About 16 fresh basil leaves, cut to chiffonade

Fine sea salt

6 swordfish steaks, 1½ to 2 inches thick

Directions

Dice the heirloom tomatoes, transferring them to a mesh colander set above a medium bowl to collect all the juices. Let them sit and drain in the colander until you have collected 1/4 to 1/3 cup of juice. Reserve tomatoes for salsa.

Whisk the lemon juice and olive oil into the tomato juice to create a thickened emulsion. Pour off half of this tomato vinaigrette into a small bowl and reserve.

Dice the avocados and fold them into the remaining liquid in the medium bowl. The acids should help delay any browning of the avocados. Fold in the reserved tomatoes, garlic, cheese and basil. Season this salsa to taste with salt.

Prepare the grill for direct grilling at about 500°F.

Rinse and dry the swordfish. Brush the reserved vinaigrette onto both sides of the steaks. Sprinkle with salt.

Grill the swordfish directly over the hottest part of the fire until the fish flakes under firm pressure, turning only once. Total cooking time should be roughly 10 to 12 minutes for 2-inch-thick steaks.

Serve the grilled fish with a few spoonfuls of the salsa on each plate.

Grilled Sea Bass with Blackberry Balsamic Reduction

Sea bass develops a wonderful, slightly sweet flavor when exposed to the heat of an open fire. The tart and acidic blackberry balsamic reduction is a perfect pairing. The presentation and flavor of this dish belies the simplicity behind its preparation.

Serves 4

For the Blackberry Balsamic Reduction

2/3 cup fresh blackberry juice plus 8 whole blackberries for garnish (start with about 11 ounces of blackberries)

1/3 cup balsamic vinegar

2½ teaspoons light-brown sugar

For the Sea Bass

2 pounds wild sea bass fillet

Extra virgin olive oil

Fine sea salt

Directions

To extract the blackberry juice, force the berries through a mesh strainer. Discard the solids. (11 ounces of blackberries should yield about 3/4 cup of juice, so you may have a little extra — perfect for Blackberry Ginger Martinis. Check *KalamazooGourmet.com* for a recipe.)

Combine the blackberry juice, balsamic vinegar and sugar in a medium skillet. Bring to a simmer and then reduce the heat to medium, stirring frequently until the volume has reduced to 1/3 cup (about 15 minutes). This not only thickens the sauce but also brings out the sweetness of the balsamic vinegar.

Transfer the blackberry-balsamic reduction to a double boiler or stainless steel bowl to keep warm over a hot water bath while you grill the fish.

Prepare the grill for direct grilling over a medium fire (about 400°F) and with a cooler or indirect zone that may be needed for perfectly cooking the fish.

Rinse the fish and pat dry with paper towels. You can cook the fish as one piece and divide it later (which makes it a little easier to grill), or you can slice the fish into four pieces prior to grilling. Lightly brush the fish with olive oil on all sides except the skin and then sprinkle with salt. Allow the fish to rise to room temperature before grilling.

Grill the fish over direct heat with the hood closed, starting with the skin-side up. Do not turn the fish until it has curled away from the grill grate. At this time, it is ready to release itself, and you can check to see if the fish is nicely browned. Once browned (at least 5 minutes and as many as 10), turn the fish over and continue grilling over direct heat with the skin-side down and the hood closed.

Unlike salmon or tuna, sea bass tastes best off the grill when it is fully cooked. Sea bass is cooked through when the meat flakes easily under pressure. It should still be moist. For thicker fillets of 1½ inches or more, you should move the fish to a lower temperature or indirect cooking zone after the first 15 minutes on the grill if it is not yet done.

Once cooked, divide the fillet onto four plates. Stir the blackberry-balsamic reduction and then drizzle over the plated fish. Garnish each with 2 fresh blackberries.

Maple-Planked Salmon with Maple Soy Glaze

A glaze that combines a soy sauce reduction with maple syrup delivers the perfect combination of sweet and savory. Great for salmon or chicken and a nice finish for grill-roasted sweet potato fries.

Serves 4

For the Maple Soy Glaze

1/4 cup soy sauce

2 tablespoons light-brown sugar

1/2 cup maple syrup

For the Planked Salmon

Maple plank(s), soaked at least 2 hours

2 pounds salmon fillet, skin removed, divided into 4 equal portions

Extra virgin olive oil

Fine sea salt

2 slices lemon, 1/4 inch thick

1 tablespoon sliced green onions

Directions

Preheat the grill for indirect cooking at about 400°F.

While the grill is heating, reduce the soy sauce in an 8-inch skillet over medium heat until thickened, about 10 minutes. Stir frequently and be very careful not to burn the sauce. Stir in the brown sugar until dissolved. Return to a simmer and stir in the maple syrup. Return to a simmer and then remove from the heat.

Lightly brush the salmon with olive oil and sprinkle with salt on both sides. Place on the plank(s) with the skinned side down. Brush the tops with the Maple Soy Glaze and place the plank(s) on the grill in the indirect zone. Cook with the hood closed. Brush the salmon with additional glaze after about 10 minutes. The total cooking time for the salmon should be about 20 minutes. The salmon is cooked when it flakes freely under gentle pressure.

Remove the salmon from the grill. Grill the lemon slices over direct heat until marked, about 1 inch per side.

Garnish each portion of salmon with 1/2 slice of grilled lemon and a sprinkle of green onion slices.

Salmon with Grapefruit Butter Sauce, Spinach and Capellini

This sauce is the "nectar of the gods!" Perhaps a bit of an exaggeration, but it is mighty good. Ben Disney, a Kalamazoo Outdoor Gourmet sales representative created the concept, and it has been a favorite of mine ever since.

If you get some overly sour grapefruit, however, it can be really sour. You may need to add some honey to the equation. With the right produce selection, reducing the grapefruit down to a syrup enhances its sweetness with just the right amount of tart left for your tongue.

Serves 4

8 to 10 large, very ripe red grapefruit

Honey, if needed

4 salmon fillets, thick portions only, 1/2 to 3/4 pound each

Extra virgin olive oil

Fine sea salt

5 quarts water

1 pound dried capellini pasta

5 ounces baby spinach leaves

7 tablespoons sweet cream butter at room temperature

Directions

This dish is best cooked with a partner who can cook the pasta and sauté the spinach while the salmon is being grilled. Otherwise, follow the instructions here for solo cooking.

To start the Grapefruit Butter Sauce, squeeze as much juice from the grapefruits as you can. You are looking for at least 4 cups of juice. Reduce the juice over medium heat in a wide pan. The wider the pan, the more surface area you have to speed the reduction. Whisk frequently, reducing the volume to about 1½ cups. Test for taste. It should be tart, but it shouldn't make you pucker. If needed, whisk in some honey until the sweet and tart are balanced the way you like. Remove from heat and reserve. The butter will be whisked in during the final moments before serving.

Prepare the grill for direct cooking at 500°F and start 5 quarts of water boiling for the pasta.

Rinse and dry the salmon. Brush with olive oil and sprinkle with salt.

Cook the pasta according to the instructions on the package, usually about 2 minutes. Drain and rinse with cold water to halt the cooking. Toss with olive oil to keep it from sticking together (if going directly from pot to plate, the rinsing step and the olive oil can be skipped).

Place the salmon on the grill directly over the fire, skin-side-up. Leave each fillet in one place until the skin starts to pull the fish away from the grill at the edges and the salmon has released itself from the surface. Turn, and continue cooking, skin-side down until the fish flakes under gentle pressure. Slide a turner between each fillet and its skin, lifting the fish off the grill and leaving the skin behind. Discard the skin.

Quickly sauté the spinach with 1 tablespoon butter in a medium chef's pan until just wilted. Toss in the pasta to combine and reheat the pasta if necessary.

To finish the Grapefruit Butter Sauce, return the grapefruit reduction to medium heat then whisk in 6 tablespoons butter until silky-smooth.

Plate the pasta, top with a salmon fillet and drizzle with the Grapefruit Butter Sauce.

Grilled Potato Salad

This potato salad was always going to be a little unconventional, but when I decided to assemble it on individual plates instead of in a single bowl, the "deconstructed" dish became much more unique. You can toss it all in a bowl for easier serving if you like. Simply cut up the bacon and eggs into small pieces and gently toss it all together.

Perfectly grilled petite potato halves are crispy on the outside and flaky-tender on the inside. The dressing is spiked with paprika and chipotle powder for a deeper flavor and a little kick, while sliced baby bell peppers deliver a bright flavor highlight.

Serves 6

For the Chipotle Dressing

1/4 cup sour cream

1/2 cup mayonnaise

1/4 teaspoon chipotle chile powder

1/4 teaspoon smoked paprika

3/4 teaspoon Colman's mustard powder

1 large clove garlic, crushed

1/4 teaspoon kosher salt

1/2 teaspoon champagne vinegar

For the Salad

3 hard- or soft-boiled eggs

3 slices bacon, cooked crisp

2 green onions, thinly sliced

6 assorted baby sweet peppers, thinly sliced (I also use 2 baby purple jalapeños for a more intense salad)

9 petite gold potatoes, halved lengthwise

9 petite red potatoes, halved lengthwise

Olive oil

Kosher salt

Directions

First, make the dressing. Combine the first 8 ingredients in a mixing bowl and whisk thoroughly. Cover and store in the refrigerator for at least 30 minutes to let the flavors meld.

Prepare the grill for indirect cooking at 500°F. While the grill is heating, prepare all of the remaining ingredients. Toss the potatoes in olive oil to coat and sprinkle liberally with salt.

Transfer the potatoes to the grill surface in the indirect zone with the cut-sides down. Close the hood and roast the potatoes until the skins are somewhat crispy and the potatoes are cooked through, about 15 minutes.

For each plate, put down 6 potato halves and drizzle with dressing. Add half an egg and half a slice of bacon. Garnish with green onions and bell peppers.

Cucumber and Tomato Salad with Grilled Corn

A perfect summer cookout deserves a perfect summery salad. Fresh produce flavors meld with lemony balsamic vinaigrette and mellow feta cheese. The salad can be prepared in advance and refrigerated for a few hours while you do other grilling.

Serves 8 to 10

3 tablespoons golden balsamic vinegar

3 tablespoons freshly squeezed lemon juice

Extra virgin olive oil

2 large cucumbers, halved lengthwise and then sliced 1/2 inch thick

2½ pounds ripe tomatoes, cut into bite-sized pieces

1 small Vidalia onion, thinly sliced

1 pound raw sheep's milk feta cheese, cubed

3 ears fresh corn, shucked, leaving the stalk intact

Kosher salt

Coarsely ground white pepper

Directions

Prepare the grill for direct grilling over medium heat.

Combine the golden balsamic, lemon juice and 6 tablespoons olive oil in a 5-quart mixing bowl. Whisk until thickened. Add the cucumbers, tomatoes, onion and feta. Gently fold together, being careful not to bruise the tomatoes. Set the bowl aside at room temperature.

Lightly brush the corn with olive oil and sprinkle with salt. Grill over direct heat, turning as soon as each side is marked by the heat. Remove from the grill and let cool until you can comfortably hold onto the stalk ends. Cut the kernels from the cobs and add to the bowl. Gently fold together and season to taste with salt and pepper. A generous amount of salt will likely be needed. Cover and refrigerate for 1 to 4 hours before serving.

Blueberry Salad with Goat Cheese and Mixed Baby Greens

Fresh blueberries are one of the best ingredients summer brings to our tables. Bursting with flavor, they are joined by caramelized pecans, mellow goat cheese and a quick and easy blueberry vinaigrette dressing.

Serves 4

For the Blueberry Vinaigrette

2 tablespoons blueberry juice from a bottle

2 tablespoons extra virgin olive oil

2 teaspoons balsamic vinegar

1½ teaspoons freshly squeezed lemon juice

For the Salad

2 to 3 ounces mixed baby greens

4 ounces goat cheese, broken into pieces or crumbled

6 ounces fresh blueberries

4 ounces caramelized pecans (use pralines if you can't find these)

Directions

Combine the first 4 ingredients in a round-bottomed bowl. Whisk vigorously until the dressing is thickened and opaque.

Divide the greens onto 4 plates. Top with blueberries, goat cheese and pecans. Re-whisk the vinaigrette and drizzle over the salads. Enjoy!

Grilled Bread Salad with Green Beans and Lemon Pepper Vinaigrette

Like a Niçoise with a lot of bread but without the tuna, this quick salad makes a perfect lunch or an ideal side dish for your grilled entrees, especially for a nice steak. Grilled bread and beans are complemented by homemade Lemon Pepper Vinaigrette, baby greens, Kalamata olives and sweet grape tomatoes.

Serves 2

For the Lemon Pepper Vinaigrette

1 tablespoon extra virgin olive oil

1 tablespoon freshly squeezed lemon juice

1 tablespoon balsamic vinegar

1/2 teaspoon cracked black pepper

For the Salad

About 8 ounces trimmed fresh green beans

1/4 cup freshly squeezed lemon juice

1/4 cup extra virgin olive oil, plus extra for brushing bread

1 teaspoon fine sea salt , plus extra for seasoning bread

2 slices rustic-style bread, frozen

1 or 2 large cloves garlic, peeled

10 to 12 Kalamata olives, pitted and slivered

About 2 ounces mixed baby greens

20 grape tomatoes, halved lengthwise

Directions

Combine the Lemon Pepper Vinaigrette ingredients in a small to medium bowl and whisk vigorously to thicken.

Combine the green beans with lemon juice, olive oil and salt in a bowl or zip-top bag. Toss occasionally to thoroughly coat and marinate while the grill is getting ready.

Prepare the grill for direct cooking at 400° to 500°F.

Remove the bread slices from the freezer and rub the garlic into each slice. While the bread is still frozen, it will act like a grater, so the garlic will really infuse the bread. Brush the slices on both sides with olive oil and sprinkle with salt.

Grill the bread over direct heat in a slightly cooler zone of the grill. Cook until the bread is nicely browned and crispy on the outside, turning once, usually about 4 minutes per side.

About 4 minutes before you expect the bread to be done, drain the green beans, discard the marinade and add the beans to the grill on your Kalamazoo "veggie" surface or in a preheated grill basket. Grill over direct heat, tossing and turning for about 4 minutes. The beans should be cooked through but still crisp.

Remove the beans and bread from the grill. Cut the bread into squares. Rewhisk the vinaigrette. Toss together the bread, beans, olives, baby greens, grape tomatoes and about half of the vinaigrette. Add more vinaigrette to your liking and serve while the green beans and bread are still warm from the grill.

Caprese Salad with Grilled Tuscan Bread

One of the best fates that can befall a tomato is to be joined by fresh mozzarella and basil in a simple salad. Adding a slice of perfectly grilled bread and a drizzle of balsamic reduction elevates the traditional Caprese salad. Reducing the balsamic intensifies the sweetness and complexity.

Serves 4

1/4 cup balsamic vinegar

4 slices Tuscan bread, about 1/2 inch thick

Extra virgin olive oil

Fine sea salt

4 slices heirloom tomato, about 1/2 inch thick

About 8 ounces fresh buffalo's milk mozzarella (ovolone size), sliced

8 large basil leaves, washed and dried without bruising

Directions

Prepare the grill for direct grilling over medium heat.

Reduce the balsamic vinegar in a wide saucepan over medium heat until very thick, about 15 minutes. A wide pan increases the surface area of the liquid to speed the reduction. Remove from heat and reserve in the saucepan.

Generously brush the bread slices with olive oil. Sprinkle liberally with good quality sea salt. Grill over direct heat until nicely marked and lightly toasted, turning once, about 3 minutes per side. It is difficult to grill it too little, but easy to grill it too much. Be careful not to let the bread dry out. Remove the bread from the grill.

Place 1 slice of bread, 1 slice of tomato, a couple slices of cheese and 2 basil leaves on each of 4 plates. Drizzle lightly with balsamic reduction. If necessary, re-heat the balsamic reduction over low heat until it is liquid enough to drizzle from a spoon. Serve with steak knives and forks.

Fennel and Grilled Blackberry Polenta Salad

What can I say? This one's a little bit out there, but I think the flavors and textures, although unusual, are great for special occasions. The visual alone makes it a star of the table. The quick and easy orange-honey dressing is appropriate for a wide variety of summer salads, and the polenta is good enough that it is worth making a double batch.

Serves 4

For the Polenta

2 cups water

1 tablespoon unsalted butter

3/4 cup polenta

3/4 teaspoon kosher salt

6 ounces blackberries, cut in half lengthwise

Extra virgin olive oil

For the Orange Honey Dressing

2 tablespoons extra virgin olive oil

2 tablespoons freshly squeezed orange juice

1 tablespoon honey, plus more for drizzling if desired

1/4 teaspoon black pepper

3 ounces fennel bulb, sliced very thin, plus the greens

Directions

The polenta needs a couple of hours to set, so start it early or make it the night before. To make the polenta, bring the water to a boil in a medium saucepan. Add the butter and stir to melt. Whisk in the polenta and salt, then return to a simmer. Reduce the heat to a low simmer and cook for 10 to 15 minutes, stirring frequently, until very thick. Fold in the blackberries and transfer the mixture to an oiled 8 x 8-inch baking dish or plastic food container. Smooth the mixture out evenly with a spatula and let it cool. Once the polenta is cooled, cover it tightly and refrigerate for at least 2 hours.

Prepare the grill for direct cooking at about 400°F.

While the grill is heating, prepare the Orange Honey Dressing by whisking together all of the ingredients.

Remove the polenta from the baking dish and slice it into large pieces, about 4 x 4 inches, so that they are easy to handle. Immediately before grilling, lightly brush both sides of each piece with olive oil.

Grill the polenta over direct heat until nicely marked and heated through, about 6 minutes per side. Remove from the grill and slice into cubes.

Gently toss together the grilled polenta, fennel and dressing. It may be best to use your hands in order to avoid breaking down the polenta too much. You might like it with a little more honey drizzled on top after plating if you find the fennel is particularly bitter.

Grilled Caesar Salad

Fire brings out the juices and softens the fibers of vegetables, and I think it adds a warmth to the flavor that is difficult to describe. As strange as it may sound to grill lettuce, this salad is a real treat for special occasions.

Serves 2

For the Caesar Dressing

1 egg

3/4 cup extra virgin olive oil

Freshly squeezed juice of 1/2 lemon

3 tablespoons champagne vinegar

1 large clove garlic, finely chopped

1/2 teaspoon fine sea salt

1/2 teaspoon dry ground mustard (Colman's)

3/4 cup shredded Parmesan cheese

For the Salad

2 frozen slices sourdough bread, 3/4-inch thick

2 garlic cloves, peeled

2 tablespoons extra virgin olive oil

2 pinches fine sea salt

1 head romaine lettuce, washed and dried, left whole (select one that is tightly formed)

2 slices bacon

2 slices tomato, 1/2-inch thick

2 anchovy fillets (optional)

Freshly ground black pepper to taste

Directions

Coddle the egg by bringing a few inches of water to a boil in a pan. Turn off the heat and lower the egg into the hot water bath on a slotted spoon. Let sit 2 minutes, then remove.

Crack the egg and combine it with the olive oil, lemon juice, vinegar, chopped garlic, 1/2 teaspoon salt, mustard and Parmesan in a blender. Blend until whipped and smooth. Refrigerate the dressing, covered, while you prepare the rest of the salad.

Prepare the grill for direct grilling at medium heat between 300° and 400°F.

Immediately upon removing the bread slices from the freezer, rub the 2 cloves of garlic into the hard surfaces of the bread. Brush with olive oil and sprinkle with 2 pinches of sea salt.

Slice the head of lettuce in half lengthwise, leaving the base attached to hold the leaves together.

Cook the bacon until brown and crisp in a skillet or, if you are comfortable doing so, directly on the grill grate. Remove and set aside on paper towels.

Place the bread and tomato slices on the grill directly over the fire. Cook the bread for roughly 2 minutes per side, until marked, and then move to a warming rack or indirect cooking zone. Cook the tomato slices for roughly 5 minutes per side, 10 minutes total.

With about 2 of the 10 minutes remaining, add the lettuce to the grill directly over the fire with the cut-side down. Grill for about 2 minutes, until nicely marked.

Remove the lettuce, tomato slices and bread from the grill. Cut the bases from the lettuce halves and discard. Transfer the lettuce halves to two plates. Cut the bread slices into croutons. Top the lettuce with the reserved dressing, croutons, tomato slices and bacon. Add 1 anchovy to each, if desired. Season to taste with pepper and serve warm with steak knives.

Asparagus Wraps with Crispy Prosciutto and Herbed Cheese

This dish makes a great appetizer or side. Crispy prosciutto wraps tender asparagus with a cheesy surprise inside.

Serves 4

1 pound (1 bunch) asparagus, medium-sized spears

1 tablespoon freshly squeezed lemon juice

1 tablespoon extra virgin olive oil

5 ounces Boursin garlic herb cheese

1 teaspoon finely grated fresh lemon zest

About 10 slices prosciutto (1 slice for every 3 asparagus spears)

Directions

Prepare the grill for direct grilling over medium-high heat, about 400°F.

Trim the toughened bases off the asparagus spears and discard, leaving each spear the same length. Whisk together the lemon juice and olive oil in a medium bowl and toss in the asparagus to thoroughly coat.

Work together the Boursin cheese and lemon zest to thoroughly combine.

Lay out a slice of prosciutto. Place three asparagus spears across the end of the slice and add a 1½ teaspoon-sized dollop of cheese mixture on the center of the asparagus. Roll tightly into the prosciutto. Repeat, rolling 3 spears into each slice of prosciutto.

Grill the wraps over direct heat, turning frequently, until the asparagus is marked and the prosciutto is crispy. Serve hot.

Green Figs Stuffed with Gorgonzola, Bacon and Walnuts

The heat of the grill caramelizes the sugars in fruit for fantastically layered flavors. This is especially true of figs because of the high sugar content. Our recipe balances the sweetness with crispy bacon, crunchy walnuts and luscious Gorgonzola cheese.

Serves 4

12 green figs

About 1/2 cup crumbled Gorgonzola cheese

About 2 ounces roasted walnuts

2 bacon slices, cooked crisp

4 short skewers (see skewer notes on page 15)

Directions

Prepare the grill for direct grilling at about 500°F.

Use a pairing knife to cut the pointed end off each fig. Insert the tip of the knife into the open end and rotate to make an opening for the stuffing. Insert a little cheese, a piece of walnut and a couple of slivers of bacon into each fig. Skewer the figs in sets of three. Do not skewer through the open ends.

Grill over direct heat, rolling the skewers once every minute or so until the figs are nicely marked on the outside and the cheese is melted on the inside. Serve hot.

Demon Toes

I've been grilling these fiery appetizers at block parties and barbecues for more than a dozen years, and they're always a huge hit. For this cookbook, however, they're taking on a new (and more apt) name. I've always called them "Hot Kisses," but frankly they are usually a little ugly coming off the grill, and they don't kiss so much as they bite. So, from now on, I am calling them "Demon Toes."

Serves 6

24 medium-sized jalapeños

7 ounces Chihuahua cheese

10 ounces imitation crabmeat flakes

4 fresh limes

24 slices center-cut bacon

24 toothpicks

Directions

Preheat the grill for direct cooking at 400° to 500°F. Make sure you also have a "safe zone" — an area of the grill with low or no heat where you can leave any troublesome Demon Toes until they settle down and can return to the fire.

Wearing latex gloves to protect your hands from the hot peppers, cut off the stem end of each jalapeño and hollow out the pepper to remove ribs and all seeds. I use the handle end of an iced-tea spoon for hollowing the peppers.

Cut the cheese into wedge-shaped sticks, sized to fit into the point of each jalapeño and fill about half of the cavity. Stuff a piece of cheese into each jalapeño. Follow with imitation crabmeat to fill the rest of each cavity. Capping the cavity with the crabmeat helps keep the cheese from melting out. Compress the stuffing into each jalapeño. For food safety reasons, all jalapeños should be stuffed with cheese and crab before handling the bacon. Squeeze a lime over the stuffed jalapeños.

Wrap each stuffed jalapeño with a strip of bacon. Start by placing one end of the bacon in the middle of the jalapeño, running lengthwise over the open end. Hold the end of the bacon against the side of the jalapeño and pull the bacon tightly up and over the open end, closing off the opening. Continue down the other side of the jalapeño to the pointed tip and then wrap around, spiraling back toward the open end. Pierce all the way through the bacon and jalapeño with a toothpick to hold it all together.

Squeeze the juice of 2 more limes over the assembled Demon Toes.

Transfer the Demon Toes to the grill. Turn occasionally until the bacon is crisp and fully cooked. Your goal is to achieve crisp bacon on the outside while the jalapeño is still somewhat firm and bright green in color.

Remove the peppers from the grill and let cool for 5 minutes. Cut the remaining lime into wedges and serve with the peppers. (Warn your guests that there is a toothpick in each piece.)

Demon Toes can be served without condiments or accompanied by your favorite ranch dressing, rémoulade or sour cream.

Tequila Baked Beans

Baked beans are one of the most traditional sides for serving with ribs, but these aren't traditional baked beans. They are a big departure from the norm. They are sweet. They can be a little spicy. And they are delicious. Tequila adds an herbaceous flavor that I am at a loss to describe. The agave nectar used instead of the more traditional molasses carries right along with the tequila theme. Try the beans with the Coffee-Rubbed Beef Back Ribs on page 27.

Serves 6 to 8

4 slices of bacon (I love using Black Forest Bacon)

1 Vidalia onion, chopped

6 cloves garlic, peeled and sliced

1 poblano pepper, stemmed, seeded and chopped

1 sweet red pepper, stemmed, seeded and chopped

1 to 3 chipotle chiles from a can (using 3 will result in a medium heat)

1/4 cup freshly squeezed lime juice

1/2 cup Milagro Silver tequila

1/2 cup raw blue agave nectar

2 teaspoons ground coffee (I suggest finely ground Illy dark roast coffee for espresso)

3/4 teaspoon kosher salt

2 cans (15 ounces each) kidney beans, rinsed and drained

1 can (15 ounces) black-eyed peas, rinsed and drained

1 cup hickory wood chips, soaked for at least an hour

1 cup hickory wood chips, dry

Directions

Prepare a grill for indirect grilling at 300°F to 325°F.

In an earthenware or cast iron Dutch oven, brown the bacon slices on both sides over medium heat. Stop short of becoming crispy. Remove the bacon and reserve. Remove all but about 2 teaspoons of fat from the Dutch oven and discard.

Add the onions and garlic to the fat and drippings remaining in the Dutch oven and cook over medium heat. Stir frequently until softened but not transparent.

Add all the remaining ingredients, except for the beans and the reserved bacon (and the wood chips, of course). Stir to thoroughly combine.

Slice the bacon into small pieces and gently stir it in along with the beans. Return to a simmer, and then transfer the Dutch oven to the indirect cooking zone of the grill. Add some of the wood chips to the grill to create smoke. If cooking with charcoal, you can add about 1/4 of the soaked and unsoaked chips directly on top of the coals. If cooking with charcoal or with gas, you can create a few smoking envelopes. Add them to the grill one at a time, spaced out during the cooking session.

Cook the beans in the uncovered Dutch oven with the grill hood closed for 2 hours. Stir the beans and add more wood chips to the fire every 30 minutes. Remove from the grill and serve.

Note: If you are also making the Coffee-Rubbed Beef Ribs on page 27, cook the beans for the first 90 minutes, and then add the ribs to the grill alongside the beans (but over the fire) for the final 30 minutes. The temperature of the fire should be just about right.

Creamed Corn Fresca

Creamed Corn Fresca is brighter in flavor and lighter in texture than is generally expected from a more typical creamed corn — not unlike Mexican street corn. Lime and sour cream are complemented by the heat of a little jalapeño and a touch of barbecue rub. The corn in this recipe is cooked "caveman style" à la Steven Raichlen for ultra-sweet results, but you can grill the corn using any technique you like.

Serves 6 to 8

6 ears corn with the husks intact

6 tablespoons sour cream

4 tablespoons unsalted butter, melted

2 teaspoons Not-So-Basic Barbecue Rub (see recipe on page 17)

1 jalapeño, seeded and finely chopped

Freshly squeezed lime juice (1/2 to 1 lime)

Salt to taste

Directions

Build a charcoal fire. Once the coals are completely ashed over and about to break down, place the corn husks directly on the bed of coals. Cook until the husks touching the coals are black, about 3 minutes. Turn the corn about 1/3 rotation and repeat. Do this one more time until most of the husk on each ear of corn is black. Remove from the grill and let rest for a minute or 2, then shuck, removing all the silk (not too difficult, as much of it has burned away at this point).

While the "caveman corn" is cooking, combine the sour cream, melted butter, barbecue rub and 1/2 jalapeño in a bowl.

Cut the corn from the cob. Stir into the sour cream mixture along with the juice of 1/2 lime. Test for taste. Add more jalapeño, more lime juice and/or salt as needed to achieve the desired balance. Serve warm.

Smoky Three-Cheese Macaroni

This is not kids' macaroni and cheese. The mahogany-colored top says it all — this is a smoky and flavorful side dish for grown-ups. The creative approach to smoking can be applied to almost any baked dish you desire… even on a gas grill.

Serves 8 to 12

1 pound dry Conchiglie pasta, cooked (you can use elbow macaroni, but I like the bigger Conchiglie)

4 tablespoons unsalted butter

4 tablespoons all purpose flour

3 cups whole milk

1/2 cup sour cream

2 large eggs

16 ounces aged Gouda cheese, shredded (I like a 9 month old Robusto for this recipe)

4 ounces Maytag blue cheese, crumbled

8 ounces medium-sharp Cheddar cheese, shredded

2 cups wood chips (I like apple for this recipe)

You will also need two aluminum turkey roasting pans and a 3-quart earthenware or cast iron casserole dish

Directions

Prepare the grill for indirect grilling at 400°F.

Cook the pasta to al dente in salted water. Drain, rinse under cold water to stop cooking and drain again.

Baked macaroni and cheese uses a classic béchamel sauce as its base. For this recipe, we are omitting the bay leaf and garlic, but sticking pretty close to this tradition. While the water for the pasta is coming to a boil, begin by making a light roux. Melt the butter in a sauce pan over medium heat. Add the flour and stir constantly with a whisk until the color is golden brown, about 5 minutes. At this point, the flour is cooked and the starchy flavor is gone. Whisk in the milk and sour cream to thoroughly combine and simmer for 5 minutes.

Beat the eggs in a small bowl (about the size of a cereal bowl). Temper the egg by adding a couple of ounces of the milk mixture to the egg bowl and stirring. Repeat several times to slowly raise the temperature of the eggs. Add the tempered eggs to the milk mixture along with the Gouda, blue cheese and 4 ounces of the Cheddar. Stir until melted in.

Transfer the drained pasta to a 3-quart casserole dish. Pour in the cheese sauce. Top with the remaining Cheddar cheese.

To create the smoking chamber, place one turkey roasting pan on the grill grate directly over the fire. Place the wood chips around the perimeter of the inside of the roaster. Close the hood and let this get started smoking for about 5 minutes. Place the casserole dish inside the aluminum roaster with the wood chips. Place the second aluminum roasting pan upside down on top as a lid, trapping in the smoke. Close the grill hood and cook for 5 to 10 minutes with the contraption still in the direct grilling zone (making sure the wood chips only smoke and do not ignite). Move the smoking contraption to the indirect zone and continue cooking for a total cooking time of 30 to 40 minutes. The top of the dish should be a deep brown color from the smoke, and the sauce should be bubbling when it is heated through. Remove the casserole dish from the roasting pans, cover tightly with foil, and wrap with towels until serving time. It should stay warm for at least 45 minutes.

Note: This smoking process will stain the outside of your casserole dish. Cast iron is your best bet, or you can use a disposable aluminum pan.

Roasted Sweet Potato Fries with Maple Soy Glaze

These simple-to-make sweet potato fries are delightfully crisp on the outside and tender on the inside. The Maple Soy Glaze adds a sweet and savory finish. The glaze is also perfect for grilled salmon.

Serves 4

2 sweet potatoes, scrubbed and cut into 8 wedges each

Extra virgin olive oil

Fine sea salt

For the Maple Soy Glaze

1/4 cup soy sauce

2 tablespoons light-brown sugar

1/2 cup maple syrup

Directions

Prepare the grill for indirect cooking at 350° to 400°F.

Brush the sweet potato wedges on all sides with olive oil and then sprinkle with salt. Transfer the wedges to the grill, placing them skin-side down in the indirect cooking zone. Cook with the hood closed, undisturbed, for about 30 minutes. Check for a crisp outer layer and tender insides. Cook for up to 15 minutes more if necessary.

While the potatoes are cooking, prepare the Maple Soy Glaze. Reduce the soy sauce in an 8-inch skillet over medium heat until thickened, about 10 minutes. Stir frequently and be very careful not to burn the sauce. Stir in the brown sugar until dissolved. Return to a simmer and stir in the maple syrup. Return to a simmer and then remove from the heat. Set aside and allow to cool and thicken.

Remove the potatoes from the grill and transfer to a serving dish or individual plates. Drizzle with the Maple Soy Glaze.

Grill-Roasted Cauliflower

There is a restaurant in downtown Kalamazoo, Michigan, that I am quite fond of called Food Dance. It specializes in using local produce, and you have its kitchen to thank for this wonderful roasted cauliflower. I never would have thought to use vegetable stock to enhance the flavor if the server at the restaurant hadn't told me their secret. Here is my recreation of this wonderful side dish, and it has become a favorite winter side dish in my home.

Serves 2

1 large head of fresh cauliflower

2 tablespoons extra virgin olive oil

1/2 teaspoon fine sea salt

1/4 teaspoon ground white pepper

2 cups alder wood chips, soaked

1/2 cup vegetable stock

1 tablespoon unsalted butter

Directions

Prepare the grill for indirect cooking at 350° to 375°F.

Remove the leaves and most of the stems from the cauliflower. Cut the florets into bite-sized pieces. Toss the cauliflower with the olive oil, salt and pepper.

Spread the cauliflower into a single layer on a grill-safe baking sheet. Place the baking sheet in the indirect cooking zone. Add the alder wood chips for smoke (learn about smoking techniques on page 5) and roast with the hood closed for about 60 minutes total, turning once, until the cauliflower is well-browned (you almost can't overdo it, short of burning the cauliflower).

With about 20 minutes remaining, place the vegetable stock in a medium saucepan. Reduce over medium heat, stirring frequently, until thickened. Whisk in the butter until melted and thoroughly combined. Keep warm.

Remove the cauliflower from the grill, once fully cooked, and toss with the reduced vegetable stock. Serve immediately.

Note: For roasting, you will need a cookie sheet or half-sheet baking sheet that is suitable for the grill. Even though we are cooking at medium temperatures, it is advisable to use cookie sheets suitable for at least 450°F maximum temperatures. Some nonstick coatings should not be used at these temperatures. I use a Silpat liner in my baking sheets that is suitable for use up to 480°F.

Grilled Brussels Sprouts

Looking for a new green to grill? Try these. I like my brussels sprouts on the crunchy side. If you prefer yours to be more tender, boil the sprouts for 4 minutes before prepping them for the grill.

Serves 4

About 40 medium brussels sprouts, washed

About 8 skewers (see skewer notes on page 15)

1/4 cup olive oil

Freshly squeezed juice of 1 lemon

2 tablespoons unsalted butter, melted

1 teaspoon coarse sea salt

Freshly ground black pepper

Directions

Prepare the grill for direct grilling at about 400°F.

Remove the stem end of each sprout and then quarter lengthwise. Skewer the quarters with each piece aligned the same way on the skewer. The spacing can be tight with each piece against the next.

Place the skewers in a rectangular baking dish and coat with the olive oil and lemon juice. Transfer the skewers from the dish to the grill grate over the fire. Cook for about 10 minutes, turning once. If the sprouts are getting too dark, move the skewers to an indirect zone and increase the cooking time by about 5 minutes.

Remove from the grill and transfer the sprouts from the skewers to a prewarmed serving bowl. Toss with melted butter and salt, breaking up the sprout quarters somewhat. Season to taste with pepper and serve.

Savory Squash Pie with Tart Apples and Sweet Onion

Onions, apples and squash meld together with Spanish cheese for a rich and hearty side dish. The subtle sweetness of the onions and squash are contrasted by the tartness of the cranberries and apples.

Serves 8

1 whole large acorn squash

2 rolled frozen pie crusts (9 inch)

2 cups grated Manchego cheese

2 Granny Smith apples, cored and thinly sliced (skins left on)

1 cup sweet onion, cut into quarters and then thinly sliced

1 cup dried cranberries

3 eggs

1 cup heavy cream

2 tablespoons light-brown sugar

1 teaspoon kosher salt

1/4 teaspoon ground white pepper

2 tablespoons sweet cream butter, cut into 6 pieces

2 cups alder wood chips, soaked

Directions

Prepare the grill for indirect cooking at 350° to 375°F.

Place the whole squash in the indirect zone with the hood closed. Cook until softened, about 45 minutes, turning once. Remove from the grill and allow to cool. You may also choose to roast the squash in an oven at the same temperature without any appreciable difference in flavor. The squash may be roasted up to an hour in advance of the rest of the pie preparation.

Cut the squash in half. Remove and discard the seeds. Remove all of the flesh from the shells and discard the shells. Slice the squash about 1/4-inch thick.

Line a 9-inch cast iron skillet or heavy ceramic pie plate with 1 pie crust. Trim off any excess at the skillet's edge. Proceed to fill the pie, beginning with a thin layer of Manchego cheese, followed by thin layers of apples, onion, squash and dried cranberries, using 1/3 of each for each layer. Repeat the layering 2 more times. The pie should be overfilled and quite tall. The filling will settle when baked.

Whisk together 2 of the eggs with the cream, sugar, salt and pepper. Pour over the pie filling. Add the pieces of butter to the top. Lay the second pie crust on top. Trim off the excess and crimp the edges all around. Cut slits into the top to vent steam. Place the skillet or pie plate on a large sheet of aluminum foil. Bring the foil up to loosely wrap the edges of the pie and help prevent the perimeter of the crust from overcooking.

Place the pie in the indirect cooking zone. Add the alder wood chips for smoke (learn about smoking techniques on page 5) and bake the pie with the hood closed for 90 minutes total, turning the pie every 30 minutes for more even baking. With 20 to 30 minutes remaining, pull the foil back away from the edges. Beat the last egg and brush about half of it onto the top pie crust and continue baking for a perfectly golden presentation.

Serve warm as a side dish.

Roasted Squash Stuffed with Wild Rice and Cranberries

A tasty side dish with a lovely presentation, stuffed acorn squash is perfect for a holiday table. Removed from the shell, a portion of the squash goes back into the dish along with wild rice, fresh sage, sautéed leeks, dried cranberries and walnuts.

Serves 4

2 medium acorn squashes

3 tablespoons unsalted butter

1/2 cup chopped fresh leeks

4 teaspoons finely chopped fresh sage

2 cups cooked wild rice

Freshly grated zest of 1 lemon

1/2 cup dried cranberries

1/4 cup chopped walnuts

1/2 teaspoon fine sea salt or kosher salt

1/2 teaspoon black pepper

Directions

Prepare the grill for indirect cooking at 350° to 375°F.

Place the whole squashes in the indirect zone with the hood closed. Cook until softened, about 45 minutes, turning once. Remove from the grill and allow to cool.

Cut the squashes in half. Remove and discard the seeds. Hollow out the squashes, reserving the flesh and leaving about 1/2 inch of the flesh all the way around. Coarsely chop the flesh you removed from the shells.

Melt the butter in a large skillet over medium heat. Add the leeks and sage, then sauté until the leeks start to become transparent. Add the rice, lemon zest, cranberries, walnuts and squash to the skillet. Stir gently to combine. Season with salt and pepper.

Spoon the rice stuffing into the hollowed-out squash shells and return to the indirect zone on the grill. Heat the filled shells with the hood closed for about 20 minutes.

Serve warm.

Grilled Red Grapes with Dark Chocolate Honey Sauce

As original an idea as it is to grill grapes, I wish I could take credit for it. The inspiration for this dish, however, came from Water Street Coffee Joint in downtown Kalamazoo, Michigan. They always have something new and tasty in their pastry case, and these were a delightful discovery. In my version, honey creates a bridge between the flavors of dark chocolate and the caramelized sugars of the grapes.

Serves 8 as a Light Dessert

2 to 3 pounds large red seedless grapes

24 short skewers (see skewer notes on page 15)

1/2 cup good quality dark chocolate chips

2 tablespoons heavy cream

4 tablespoons honey

Directions

Prepare the grill for direct grilling at about 500°F.

Skewer the grapes, 5 to 6 grapes per skewer.

In a double boiler over moderate heat, melt the chocolate together with the cream. Whisk in the honey until smooth. Turn off the heat but leave the chocolate sauce in the double boiler over the hot water.

Grill the grape skewers over direct heat until blistered and hot through.

Remove the grapes from the grill, plate and drizzle with chocolate sauce. Serve warm.

Honey-Caramelized Peaches with Vanilla Mascarpone Ice Cream

You can thank Chef Alton Brown for inspiring this dish with his Honey Plums, but the Vanilla Mascarpone Ice Cream may just be the real star here. The cold ice cream plays off the warm peaches in the same way the richness of the cheese is a counterpoint to the brightness of the fruit flavors.

Serves 6

1 cup Mascarpone cheese (8 ounces)

2 cups whole milk

1/2 cup sugar

Freshly-grated nutmeg (about 1/4 of an average-size seed)

Seeds scraped from one vanilla bean

About 1/2 cup wildflower honey

6 peaches, quartered, pits removed

Directions

Combine the first 5 ingredients in a medium bowl. Whisk vigorously until the cheese is incorporated and the sugar dissolved.

Add the mixture to your ice cream maker and follow the manufacturer's instructions to make the ice cream. When finished, chill in the freezer until it hardens sufficiently. This may require a couple of hours, so make your ice cream in advance.

Cover the bottom of a 14-inch skillet with honey. Warm the honey over medium heat and add the peaches with one of the cut sides down. Raise the heat to medium-high and cook the peaches for 5 to 7 minutes without turning them. The cooked side should be slightly browned when you turn them. Turn each slice onto the other cut side and continue cooking for about another 4 minutes.

Serve the warm peaches with the cold ice cream.

Grilled Figs over Vanilla Gelato

Although not exactly common grill fare, figs are fantastic over an open flame. The fire brings out the sugars and emphasizes the sweetness. A dusting of sugar and cinnamon caramelizes the outside to turn these figs into a light dessert.

Serves 8

1/2 cup light-brown sugar

1/2 teaspoon ground cinnamon

1/4 teaspoon ground nutmeg

1/4 teaspoon cayenne pepper

Pinch salt

16 black mission figs, stems removed and halved

1 tablespoon canola oil

4 to 8 skewers (see skewer notes on page 15)

Vanilla gelato (or ice cream)

Honey (optional)

Directions

Prepare the grill for direct grilling over medium heat (about 300° to 350°F).

Combine the sugar, cinnamon, nutmeg, cayenne and salt in a small bowl.

Gently toss the figs in another bowl with the canola oil, then thread onto skewers.

Place the fig skewers on a cutting board or baking sheet and sprinkle both sides with the sugar mixture.

Cook the fig skewers directly over a medium fire, cut-side down. Cook until the sugars have completely caramelized, about 3 minutes, and then turn to cook the skin side for 2 to 3 minutes more. Be careful not to burn the figs, especially on the skin side.

Dish the gelato into 8 serving bowls and top with 4 fig halves each. Optionally drizzle with honey.

Smoke-Roasted Apple Bake with Tart Cherries

Casual, simple and delicious — baked apples come off the grill infused with apple wood smoke flavor. Baking and serving in individual dishes will delight your guests.

Serves 6

2 cups apple wood chips, soaked for at least 1 hour

1 egg

1 cup heavy cream

2 teaspoons vanilla extract

1 cup light-brown sugar

3 tablespoons all purpose flour

1/4 teaspoon ground nutmeg

1/4 teaspoon ground cloves

Unsalted butter

6 small cast iron skillets, about 3½ inches in diameter

4 Braeburn apples with the skins left on, cored and sliced in 16ths

1/4 cup dried tart cherries

1/4 cup sliced almonds

Directions

Prepare the grill for indirect grilling with wood smoke at 300°F. Also prepare a foil smoking envelope with the wood chips (see page 5).

In a medium-sized mixing bowl, beat the egg. Whisk in the cream and vanilla, and then the sugar, flour, nutmeg and cloves.

Butter the 6 individual skillets. Intermingle the apples, dried cherries and almonds into each skillet. Pour the egg mixture into the skillets until each is about 2/3 full.

Place the skillets in the indirect cooking zone and bake in the grill at 300°F for 1 hour. Rotate the skillets twice during this time. The grill hood should remain closed as much as possible, and the skillets should remain uncovered, letting the apple wood smoke infuse itself into the ingredients.

Remove from the grill and let cool for at least 10 minutes before serving in the individual skillets.

Note: This same recipe can be prepared in a single, medium-sized skillet if you do not have small ones available.

White Wine Pizza Dough

Making pizza dough from scratch really isn't a lot of work. I used to dig out the mixer and use the dough hook for kneading, but the dough actually doesn't need to be worked enough to bother with the mixer. Since I started kneading the dough by hand right in the mixing bowl, I've been making dough from scratch more often.

Yields 28 ounces of dough, enough for two 14-inch pizzas

3/4 cup warm water

Pinch of sugar

3 teaspoons active dry yeast

1/4 cup white wine, at room temperature

1¼ teaspoons kosher salt

2 tablespoons olive oil, plus extra for coating

3 cups bread flour

2 teaspoons honey

Directions

Put 6 tablespoons of the lukewarm (100° to 110°F) water, sugar and yeast in a small bowl, mix well and set aside for 5 minutes or until frothy.

In a large bowl, whisk together the remaining water with the white wine, salt and 2 tablespoons olive oil. Use a wooden spoon to stir in 1 cup of the flour, creating a batter. Stir the honey and the yeast mixture into the batter.

Add the remaining flour and continue stirring with the wooden spoon for a few minutes. Knead the mixture in the bowl until smooth and relatively firm. Clean the sides of the bowl, oil the dough with a little more olive oil and cover the bowl with a towel.

Let rise for 45 minutes. A good tip is to run a load of dishes in the dishwasher while the dough rises right above the washer door. The warm, moist air helps with the rising.

After 45 to 60 minutes, punch the dough down, split in half or quarters, knead again briefly and let rest 15 minutes more before rolling into pizza crusts. Unused dough may be frozen. Makes enough for a pair of 14-inch round pizzas or 4 individual pizzas. For more pizzas, make the dough 1 batch at a time rather than multiplying the recipe.

Note: Use this recipe for the dough in all of the pizzas that follow. Each calls for a half batch (with the exception of the deep-dish pizza), so this recipe yields enough for 2 pizzas.

Rustic Pizza with Baby Arugula, Pancetta and Tomatoes

This pizza is colorful and delicious. Grape tomatoes lend a sweet flavor to complement the salty pancetta, or you can use a variety of heirloom cherry tomatoes for a more colorful presentation. The pizza in the photo uses a combination of green zebra, black cherry, sun gold, yellow pear and grape tomatoes.

Yields One 14-inch Pizza

1/2 batch White Wine Pizza Dough, about 14 ounces (see page 133)

Cornmeal

1 cup shredded fontina cheese

1/2 cup baby arugula leaves

About 1 cup halved sweet grape tomatoes

2 ounces pancetta (rolled Italian bacon), chopped and cooked until crisp

Directions

Prepare the dough 2 hours ahead.

Preheat a pizza stone on the grill to about 500°F in the indirect cooking zone for about an hour (see page 5 for more information) or prepare your pizza oven.

Roll out or form the dough to 14 inches and transfer to a pizza prep peel dusted with cornmeal. Sprinkle the cheese evenly over the dough. Add the arugula, then the tomatoes, and then sprinkle the pancetta over the top.

Transfer to the preheated oven or pizza stone and bake for about 10 minutes or until the crust is crisp and the cheese is browning.

Note: A peel is the long-handled spadelike instrument used by bakers to slide pizzas into and out of the oven. It comes in wood or aluminum. My favorite peel for sliding pizzas into the oven is a large, rectangular aluminum tool with perforations. The perforations reduce the amount of cornmeal or flour on the bottom of the crust and make it easier for the dough to slide. Once the pizza is in the oven, I use a smaller (about 6 inches) round peel to rotate the pizza and check the bottom of the crust.

Grilled Vegetable Pizza

Celebrate summer produce with a delicious vegetable pizza. Zucchini, yellow squash and red onions all take on a roasted flavor over the open flame of the grill. A quick red sauce brings fresh tomatoes to the party.

Yields One 14-inch Pizza

1/2 batch White Wine Pizza Dough, about 14 ounces (see page 133)

1/2 zucchini squash

1/4 yellow squash

1/4 red onion

Extra virgin olive oil

Kosher salt

Cornmeal

2 ounces (1/4 cup) Fresh Tomato Red Sauce (recipe follows)

3 ounces Scamorza cheese, shredded

Fresh Tomato Red Sauce

2 1/2 pounds Roma tomatoes, roughly chopped

6 cloves garlic

1 teaspoon kosher salt

2 tablespoons extra virgin olive oil

Combine the tomatoes, garlic, salt and 2 tablespoons olive oil in a blender or food processor. Thoroughly process until the liquid is smooth and frothy. Transfer to a large saucepan. Bring to a simmer over medium heat and reduce to a thick sauce. Store any extra sauce in the refrigerator in an air-tight container for up to 4 days. Yields about 1½ cups.

Directions

Prepare the dough 2 hours ahead.

Prepare the grill for direct grilling over a hot fire. A charcoal fire is preferred for grilling the vegetables because of its drier heat characteristics.

Quarter both types of squash lengthwise. Slice the onion into narrow wedges. Pierce toothpicks through the layers of the onion to help keep the wedges together on the grill. Brush all with olive oil and sprinkle generously with kosher salt.

Grill the vegetables over the hot fire until nicely marked. The pieces will continue to cook on the pizza, so pull them off the grill before they are fully tender. Slice both types of squash into smaller pieces for the pizza. Separate the layers of the onion wedges.

Preheat a pizza stone on the grill to about 500°F in the indirect cooking zone for about an hour (see page 5 for more information) or prepare your pizza oven.

Roll out or form the dough to 14 inches and transfer to a pizza prep peel dusted with cornmeal. Spread on the sauce (a 2-ounce ladle is a handy tool if you make pizzas often), sprinkle on the cheese and distribute the vegetables.

Bake the pizza until the crust is golden brown and the toppings are hot. At 500°F it should take about 10 minutes.

Blackened Chicken Pizza

I rarely have a party without baking a couple of pizzas. They taste fantastic and set a casual tone. They also offer great opportunity for creativity. This recipe is a prime example. The mild heat from roasted poblanos and blackened chicken is tempered by the crème fraîche. The simple combination of flavors allows the smoked Cheddar to shine.

Yields One 14-inch Pizza

1/2 batch White Wine Pizza Dough, about 14 ounces (see page 133)

1 chicken breast, butterflied

About 2 teaspoons Aromatic Blackening Rub (see recipe page 75)

1 poblano pepper

Cornmeal

2 tablespoons crème fraîche

3 ounces grated smoked Cheddar cheese

Directions

Prepare the dough 2 hours ahead.

The blackened chicken and roasted poblano can be prepared ahead and refrigerated until pizza-making time.

Prepare the grill for direct grilling at 500° to 600°F.

Coat the chicken breast with blackening rub, pressing it into the surface. Grill the breast over direct heat, turning once, about 3 minutes per side or until cooked to about three-quarters doneness (the chicken will finish cooking on the pizza). Remove from the grill, slice thinly on the bias and reserve.

Grill the poblano over direct heat, turning occasionally until the skin is black. Remove from the grill and let cool in a sealed paper bag or in a bowl covered with a plate. Use a knife to scrape off and discard the charred skin. Remove and discard the stem and seed pod, then cut the pepper into 1/4 x 1 inch strips. Reserve.

Preheat a pizza stone on the grill to about 500°F in the indirect cooking zone for about an hour (see page 5 for more information) or prepare your pizza oven.

Roll out or form the dough to 14 inches and transfer to a pizza prep peel dusted with cornmeal. Spread the crème fraîche over the dough. Add the roasted poblano on top of that and then the Cheddar cheese. Finish assembling the pizza with a final layer of the reserved sliced chicken.

Bake the pizza until the crust is golden brown and the toppings are hot.

Fiery Barbecue Chicken Pizza

I call it "Fiery" not only because it brings the heat, but also because of the smoky flavors of chipotle chiles and the fire-marked corn. This pizza is loaded with flavor.

Yields One 14-inch Pizza

1/2 batch White Wine Pizza Dough, about 14 ounces (see page 133)

1/4 red onion, cut into narrow wedges

1 ear of corn, shucked

1 boneless, skinless chicken breast, butterflied

Olive oil

Kosher salt

Cornmeal

About 3 ounces (1/4 cup plus 2 tablespoons) Chipotle Barbecue Sauce (recipe follows)

2 ounces Monterey Jack cheese, shredded

1 ounce Scamorza cheese, shredded

1 serrano chile, thinly sliced

About 12 fresh cilantro leaves

Chipotle Barbecue Sauce

7.5 ounces canned chipotle chiles in adobo sauce (use the sauce and chiles)

2 Roma tomatoes, roughly chopped

6 ounces tomato paste

1½ cups light-brown sugar

3 tablespoons molasses

3 tablespoons balsamic vinegar

1 clove garlic

Combine all ingredients in a blender or food processor. Thoroughly process until liquefied. Test for the right balance of sweetness and spice, adding more brown sugar if needed. The flavor of this sauce is quite intense and is meant to be an accompaniment used in small quantities. Yields 2½ cups. Store extra sauce in the refrigerator for up to 7 days.

Directions

Prepare the dough 2 hours ahead.

Prepare the grill for direct grilling over a hot fire.

Skewer each onion wedge with a toothpick to help keep it together on the grill. Brush the onion, corn and chicken with olive oil and season liberally with kosher salt. Set aside 1 ounce of the barbecue sauce for basting the chicken.

Quickly grill the chicken, about 3 minutes per side. Do not over-cook it, because it will be cooked some more on the pizza. After grilling the first side and turning it over, brush on 1 tablespoon of the barbecue sauce. After the second side is marked by the fire, turn the chicken again and brush 1 tablespoon of the barbecue sauce on the second side. Briefly grill the second side to caramelize the sauce.

Grill the onion on both sides until nicely marked and starting to get tender. Grill the corn until well-marked all around.

Slice the chicken, cut the kernels from the cob, and separate the layers of the onion wedges.

Preheat a pizza stone on the grill to about 500°F in the indirect cooking zone for about an hour (see page 5 for more information) or prepare your pizza oven.

Roll out or form the dough to 14 inches and transfer to a pizza prep peel dusted with cornmeal. Spread on 2 ounces of Chipotle Barbecue Sauce (a 2-ounce ladle is a handy tool if you make pizzas often), sprinkle on the cheese and distribute the chicken, corn, onion and serrano.

Bake the pizza until the crust is golden brown and the toppings are hot. At 500 degrees it should take about 10 minutes.

Top with fresh cilantro before serving.

Note: For less spicy palates, you can try halving the amount of chipotles and serrano.

Avocado, Goat Cheese and Heirloom Tomato Appetizer Pizza

This appetizer pizza is light and refreshing on a warm and sunny day. Mild goat cheese and buttery avocado are complimented by the bright flavors of fresh tomato and tart lemon juice.

Yields One 14-inch Pizza

1/2 batch White Wine Pizza Dough, about 14 ounces (see page 133)

Cornmeal

Freshly squeezed juice of 1/2 lemon

1½ medium avocados, ripe (see note)

1 teaspoon fine sea salt

2 teaspoons extra virgin olive oil

1 large heirloom tomato, sliced (I used a Paul Robeson variety, or substitute about 1 cup halved sweet grape tomatoes)

2 ounces soft goat cheese

Freshly cracked black pepper

Directions

Prepare the dough 2 hours ahead.

Preheat a pizza stone on the grill to about 500°F in the indirect cooking zone for about an hour (see page 5 for more information) or prepare your pizza oven.

Roll out or form the dough to 14 inches. Transfer to a pizza prep peel dusted with cornmeal before preparing the avocado mixture.

Squeeze the lemon juice into a glass or other nonreactive bowl. Slice the avocados into the bowl and stir immediately to coat. The citric acid will help prevent the avocados from browning. Add the salt and olive oil to the mixture and mash until it is the consistency of guacamole.

Spread the avocado mixture onto the pizza dough and then top with the sliced tomatoes. Add pieces of goat cheese in the spaces between the tomatoes. Season with pepper.

Transfer to the preheated oven or pizza stone and bake until the crust is cooked and nicely browned around the edges.

Note: The best tip I know for selecting ripe avocados comes from Chef Rick Bayless. The color of an avocado is a good clue to how ripe it is (Haas avocados are usually turning black when they are ripe) but is not always reliable. To select perfect avocados, press your thumb gently into the base of the avocado. The avocado should yield somewhat but resist enough that it doesn't feel mushy. Because the base of the avocado is the last to ripen, one that yields to gentle pressure is ready to use right away without being overripe.

Grape and Ricotta Pizza with Thyme, Bacon and Honey

This pizza became an instant favorite with the neighbors and makes a great appetizer. Smoky bacon, sweet honey and savory thyme all work together with the fruity flavor from the red grapes. A little bit of sea salt brings it home.

Yields One 14-inch Pizza

1/2 batch White Wine Pizza Dough, about 14 ounces (see page 133)

Cornmeal

1/4 cup high-quality ricotta cheese (I use Miceli's)

Honey

Pinch of fine sea salt

1 teaspoon fresh thyme leaves

2 slices cooked bacon, cut into 1/2-inch pieces

12 large, red seedless grapes, halved

Directions

Prepare the dough 2 hours ahead.

Preheat a pizza stone on the grill to about 500°F in the indirect cooking zone for about an hour (see page 5 for more information) or prepare your pizza oven.

Roll out or form the dough to 14 inches and transfer to a pizza prep peel dusted with cornmeal. Spread the ricotta over the dough. Drizzle with honey. A little will go a long way. Start with just a couple of teaspoons and adjust to taste. Sprinkle on the thyme leaves and sea salt. Distribute the bacon on top.

Bake the pizza until the crust is golden brown and the toppings are hot. At 500 degrees it should take about 10 minutes. Add the grapes, cut-side down, to the pizza for the final 2 or three minutes of cooking.

Deep-Dish Three-Cheese Sausage Pizza

If you like lasagna, you'll love this Chicago-style pizza.

Yields one 12-inch pizza

1 batch White Wine Pizza Dough, about 28 ounces (see page 133)

2 pounds fresh Roma tomatoes

4 cloves garlic

1/2 teaspoon kosher salt

12 ounces scarmoza cheese, shredded

8 ounces ricotta

1 teaspoon fresh thyme leaves

12 ounces fresh mozzarella (Ovolone size), drained and dried in a mesh strainer

About 1/2 pound Italian pork sausage, casings removed and broken into small pieces

You will also need a cooling rack and a 12-inch heavy aluminum pizza pan, 2 inches deep. It should be made from at least 14 gauge material.

Directions

Prepare the dough 2 hours ahead.

Prepare the grill for indirect grilling at 400°F

Combine the tomatoes, garlic and salt in a blender and puree until very smooth. Transfer to a saucepan. Reduce over medium heat, stirring frequently until thickened into a sauce. Set aside.

Form the dough into a large circle, larger than the pizza pan and only 1/4 inch thick. The outer perimeter can be thicker. Place it over the pan and let it sag into position. Coax it into the corners of the pan, leaving the dough hanging over the edges.

Spread the scarmoza cheese into a bottom layer on the dough. Place the pizza pan with the dough and scarmoza in the indirect grilling zone and close the grill hood. Cook until the cheese is fully-melted. This helps pre-crisp the crust, and the melted cheese forms a protective layer that helps prevent the crust from becoming soggy. Remove from the grill using gloves or oven mitts.

Layer in the ricotta cheese, followed by the thyme leaves and the fresh mozzarella, keeping the layers as level as possible. Ladle on the tomato sauce and then add the sausage. Use small pieces, evenly-spaced to help ensure the raw sausage will cook fully.

With all the ingredients in the pizza pan, the pan should be only halfway full. The toppings will expand when cooking. Fold in the crust that is hanging over the edge of the pan, getting it all inside the pan, but keeping it high on the sides. If any pizza toppings overflow the sides of the crust, the pizza will be soggy.

Put the pizza pan back in the indirect grilling zone and close the grill hood. Cook for at least 40 minutes, rotating every 10 minutes. The toppings should be bubbling, the sausage should be fully cooked and the edges of the crust should be dark.

Remove from the grill and let rest 10 minutes before cutting and serving.

Zucchini Pizza Pinwheels

A lot like a calzone but with a beautiful presentation, these pizza pinwheels are wonderful starters for parties. Fresh zucchini melds with Spanish cheese and sweetened tomatoes.

Serves 4

1/2 batch White Wine Pizza Dough, about 14 ounces (see page 133)

1 cup grape tomatoes, quartered

1 tablespoon light-brown sugar

1 cup shredded zucchini (1 fresh zucchini should provide enough)

1 cup shredded Manchego cheese

1/2 teaspoon fine sea salt

Cornmeal

1 egg, beaten (optional)

Directions

Prepare the dough 2 hours ahead.

Preheat a pizza stone on the grill to about 450°F in the indirect cooking zone for about an hour (see page 5 for more information) or prepare your pizza oven.

Stir together the grape tomatoes with the brown sugar in a small bowl and let sit for at least 15 minutes.

Spread out the shredded zucchini on a large cutting board and let it air-dry for 15 minutes.

Discard the liquid in the tomato bowl and combine the tomatoes, zucchini, cheese and salt in a large bowl.

Roll out the pizza dough into a square about 15 inches to a side. Trim the large dough into four smaller perfect squares, then roll those thinner until they are each roughly 8 inches to a side.

Start with one square. Stretch the corners to elongate them, making the dough into a four-pointed star. Transfer to a pizza peel dusted with cornmeal. Spoon the zucchini filling onto the dough in a square shape that is on a diagonal to the four-pointed star. Lift two opposing corners of the star to the middle, folding over the filling, then firmly press them together between your fingers to join at the middle. Repeat with the other two corners and then press the four corners together at the middle.

Repeat to make a total of 4 pinwheels on your pizza peel. If desired, lightly brush the top of the dough with the beaten egg for more golden crusts.

Transfer the pinwheels to the pizza oven and bake until golden brown on top and cooked through, about 15 minutes.

Squash and Red Onion Pizza with Hazelnuts and Ricotta

This pizza is not one of the most beautiful creations, but it is one of the tastiest. A thin crust is topped first with a mixture of ricotta cheese, olive oil and lemon zest, and then with red onions and butternut squash caramelized with balsamic vinegar. Roasted hazelnuts provide the perfect finish.

Yields One 14-inch Pizza

1/2 batch White Wine Pizza Dough, about 14 ounces (see page 133)

1/2 butternut squash, sliced 1/4-inch thick and then cut into 1/4-inch strips

1/2 red onion, thinly sliced

Balsamic vinegar

Extra virgin olive oil

Fine sea salt

1/3 cup shelled hazelnuts, cracked

1/2 cup ricotta cheese

Finely grated zest of 1/2 lemon

About 20 very fresh (soft) rosemary leaves

Cornmeal

Directions

Prepare the dough 2 hours ahead.

Preheat a pizza stone on the grill to about 500°F in the indirect cooking zone for about an hour (see page 5 for more information) or prepare your pizza oven.

If using the grill for making the pizza, pre-heat your indoor oven to 400°F. Otherwise, prepare the grill for indirect cooking at the same temperature for roasting the squash and onion.

Spread the onion and squash in a single layer on a cookie sheet covered in parchment. Drizzle with balsamic vinegar and olive oil and sprinkle with salt. Roast at 400°F (in the oven or the indirect zone of the grill) until caramelized, about 30 minutes, turning once.

With a cooktop burner, toast the hazelnuts in a small pan over medium heat until browned and crunchy. Toss with a little sea salt and reserve.

In a small bowl, combine the ricotta, lemon zest and rosemary leaves with a little olive oil and salt to taste.

Roll out or form the dough to 14 inches and transfer to a pizza peel dusted with cornmeal. Spread the cheese mixture over the dough. Sprinkle the caramelized squash and onions over the cheese and then add the hazelnuts.

Bake the pizza until the crust is golden brown and the toppings are hot, about 10 minutes.

Mixed Berry Pizza

This pizza is almost like an upside down cobbler and makes a perfect finish to a summer pizza party. Blackberries, blueberries and raspberries blend with a creamy mixture of Mascarpone and crème fraîche with a touch of honey.

Yields One 14-inch Pizza

1/2 batch White Wine Pizza Dough, about 14 ounces (see page 133)

3 tablespoons crème fraîche

1 tablespoon Mascarpone cheese

Cornmeal

1 to 2 teaspoons honey

3 ounces mixed fresh blackberries, raspberries and blueberries

Pinch of fine sea salt

Fresh mint leaves

Directions

Prepare the dough 2 hours ahead.

Preheat a pizza stone on the grill to about 500°F in the indirect cooking zone for about an hour (see page 5 for more information) or prepare your pizza oven.

Combine the crème fraiche and Mascarpone cheese in a bowl.

Roll out or form the dough to 14 inches and transfer to a pizza prep peel dusted with cornmeal. Spread on the crème fraîche mixture. Drizzle with honey. Sprinkle with salt. Break up the raspberries and blackberries, removing and discarding the cores from the blackberries. Distribute all the berries evenly across the pizza.

Bake the pizza until the crust is golden brown and the toppings are hot. At 500 degrees it should take about 10 minutes.

Garnish with mint leaves before serving.

Pear Dessert Pizza with Praline Pecans

I can't think of a better finale for a successful pizza party than this wonderful dessert. The combination of fresh pears, crème fraîche and praline pecans is not too heavy, not too sweet, and very satisfying. Slicing the pears paper-thin allows them to just cook through without losing their texture.

Yields One 14-inch Pizza

1/2 batch White Wine Pizza Dough, about 14 ounces (see page 133)

4 ounces crème fraîche

4 teaspoons light-brown sugar

1½ Anjou pears

1/4 cup raisins

1/3 cup praline pecans, very coarsely chopped

Cornmeal

Directions

Prepare the dough 2 hours ahead.

Preheat a pizza stone on the grill to about 500°F in the indirect cooking zone for about an hour (see page 5 for more information) or prepare your pizza oven.

Combine the crème fraîche and sugar in a bowl.

Core the pears and slice paper-thin (see mandolin recommendation below) to help them cook quickly. You can peel them first, but I prefer to leave the skins on.

Roll out or form the dough to 14 inches and transfer to a pizza prep peel dusted with cornmeal. Layer the pear slices on the pizza, loosely folding each slice over on itself for a more airy pizza. Add the raisins and pralines and then drizzle the crème fraîche mixture over the top.

Transfer to the preheated pizza stone and bake for about 15 minutes until the crust is crisp and the edges of the pears are browning.

Note: After years of frustration with my old mandolin, I finally found an adjustable mandolin from Kyocera that is easy to use, easy to clean and stays sharper longer thanks to its ceramic blade (see picture). The pears in this dessert pizza were quickly and easily sliced to just .5 mm thick. It has become an essential tool in my kitchen.

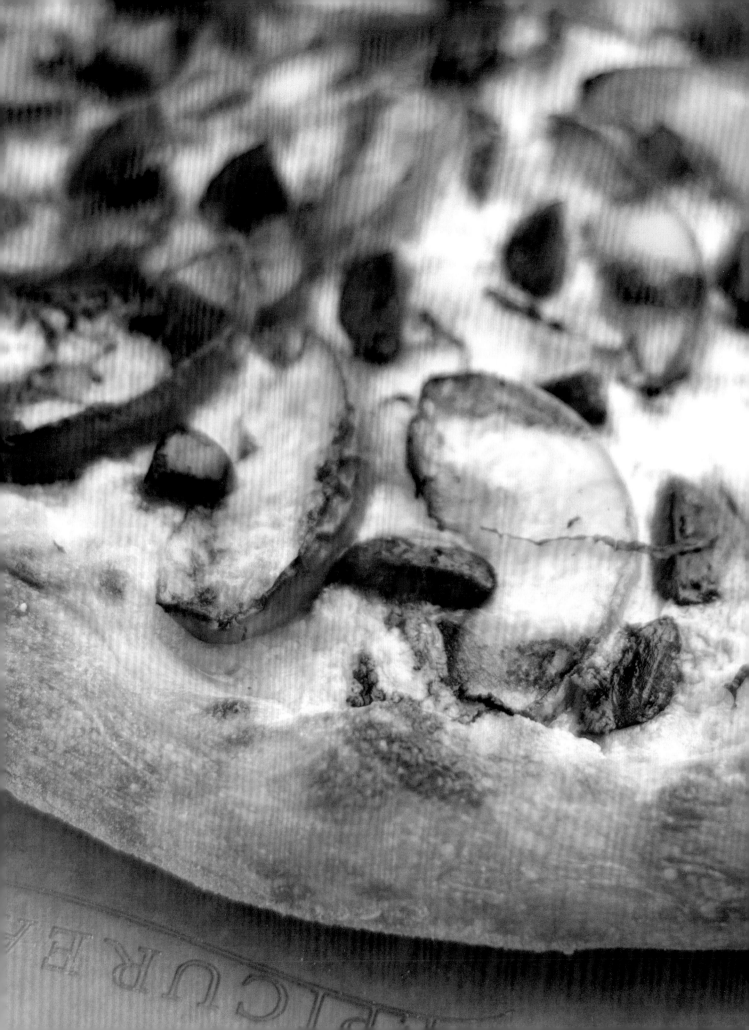

Sweet Peach Pizza with Tart Cherries

Here is another fantastic dessert pizza for outdoor parties. The sweetness of peaches, quickly caramelized on the grill, is balanced by tart cherries while the whole pizza is mellowed on a rich foundation of Mascarpone cheese. This is a must-try next time fresh peaches and cherries are in season.

Yields One 14-inch Pizza

1/2 batch White Wine Pizza Dough, about 14 ounces (see page 133)

2 yellow peaches, sliced about 1/4-inch thick

4 ounces Mascarpone cheese

1½ teaspoons light-brown sugar

1/2 teaspoon freshly squeezed lemon juice

Cornmeal

4 mint leaves, thinly sliced

7 tart cherries, pitted and sliced

Directions

Prepare the dough 2 hours ahead.

Preheat a pizza stone on the grill to about 500°F in the indirect cooking zone for about an hour (see page 5 for more information) or prepare your pizza oven.

Grill the peach slices directly over a medium fire for about 1 minute per side to enhance the sweetness.

Stir together the Mascarpone, sugar and lemon juice in a small bowl.

Roll out or form the dough to 14 inches and transfer to a pizza peel dusted with cornmeal.

Spread the Mascarpone mixture over the prepared dough. Sprinkle half of the mint leaves evenly over the cheese mixture. Add the peach slices in a single layer with enough space in between to sprinkle cherries. Add the cherries.

Bake the pizza until the crust is golden brown and the toppings are hot, about 10 minutes. Sprinkle the remaining mint leaves over the top and let the pizza rest for a few minutes before slicing.

Skillet Cornbread with Chiles, Corn and Cheddar

Many people acknowledge that you can bake on a grill, but most of them believe it is too much work to bother with. Using a charcoal or hybrid grill as a wood-fired oven is not only worth it but is quite easy to do as well. Adding wood smoke with indirect cooking techniques on a typical gas grill also can work.

Like most cornbread recipes, this one is very forgiving in its baking requirements, and it provides a great opportunity to try your hand at baking on the grill.

Serves 6 to 8

1 or 2 poblano chiles, depending on whether you want mild or medium cornbread

2 ears corn, shucked

2 cups stone-ground cornmeal

2/3 cup all-purpose flour

1 teaspoon baking powder

1/2 teaspoon baking soda

1/2 teaspoon blackening spice blend

1 teaspoon kosher salt

2 eggs

3 tablespoons honey

2 cups buttermilk

2 tablespoons vegetable oil

1/2 cup shredded mild Cheddar cheese

1 tablespoon unsalted butter

Directions

Prepare the grill for indirect cooking at a target temperature of 400°F. A wood fire is best. For a gas fire, add a small amount of wood chips for a subtle smoke flavor when the cornbread goes onto the grill (see smoking techniques on page 5). Preheat a cast iron skillet in the indirect cooking zone.

Quickly roast the poblano(s) over direct heat on the hottest part of the grill. Turn them occasionally until all sides of the skin are blackened and blistered. Transfer from the grill to a paper bag. Close the bag and let the poblano(s) steam in the bag for at least 5 minutes.

Quickly grill the ears of corn over direct heat until they are nicely marked on all sides. Remove from the grill while the corn is still crisp and barely cooked, about 3 minutes.

Whisk together the next 6 ingredients in a large bowl. In a separate bowl, beat the eggs and then whisk in the honey, buttermilk and vegetable oil.

Cut the corn from the cobs and separate the kernels. Scrape the burnt skin off the poblano(s) and discard along with the seeds. Finely dice the poblano flesh.

Once the grill is at a steady 400°F in the indirect zone, add the buttermilk and egg mixture to the cornmeal mixture. Stir until moist. Do not overmix. Stir in the corn, poblanos and cheese.

Add the butter to the preheated skillet and spread around to coat the bottom and sides. Pour in the cornbread batter and bake with the grill hood closed until the center is cooked through, about 30 minutes.

Let cool for at least 10 minutes, then slice and serve.

Grilled Naan

Fresh flatbreads are easy to make, fun to grill and a real treat at the table. Try them for sandwiches and burgers, as a pizza crust, or simply serve them at the table as bread.

Yields 8 Naan

2 teaspoons active dry yeast

1½ cups water, lukewarm

4 cups bread flour, plus more for dusting and rolling

2 teaspoons salt

2 teaspoons sugar

Pinch of baking soda

1/4 cup plus 1 tablespoon (5 tablespoons) plain Greek-style yogurt, at room temperature

1/4 cup extra virgin olive oil, plus more for coating the dough

Directions

Stir the yeast into 3 tablespoons of the lukewarm (100° to 110°F) water. Let it sit for about 5 minutes. It should be frothy by the end of this time.

Combine the 4 cups flour, salt, sugar and baking soda in a medium mixing bowl. Add the yogurt, 1/4 cup oil, remaining water and the yeast mixture. It is important that the yogurt be room temperature. If it is cold, you risk killing the yeast.

Use your hands to first mix the dry and wet ingredients together and then knead well for about 2 minutes. The dough should be soft but not too sticky. Cover the bowl with a warm towel and let the dough rise for about 90 minutes. A good tip is to run a load of dishes in the dishwasher while the dough rises right above the washer door. The warm, moist air helps with the rising.

After 90 minutes, the dough should have doubled in volume. If it hasn't risen quite that much, don't worry. Divide the dough and roll into 8 equal balls. Lightly coat the dough balls with oil and let rise for 30 more minutes under a warm, damp towel. Meanwhile, prepare the grill for direct grilling over high heat, around 600°F.

Dust each dough ball with flour and use a rolling pin to roll into a flat oval about 1/8 inch thick. They should be very thin. If you roll the dough directly on your countertop without too much flour, you can use the slight stickiness to help stretch the dough. I find it easiest to roll one flatbread and then grill it before rolling the next. If you have help, form a production line.

Lay the rolled dough directly on the grill grate over a hot fire. There should be no need to oil the dough so long as the grate is clean and hot. Within 1 minute of hitting the grill, the dough should begin to bubble. Once the entire top surface has bubbled, it is time to flip the flatbread. Use tongs to do so. Grill the second side for about half the time of the first side and then remove from the grill. The total cooking time is typically less than 2 minutes. Repeat this process until all 8 flatbreads are cooked and then set them aside.

If serving grilled sandwiches or burgers, you can grill the naan immediately before grilling the meat or other ingredients, and they will be warm when you serve the sandwiches. Or you can make the naan ahead of time and then quickly reheat them on the grill.

Food Temperature Chart

Beef Steaks	Gourmet	USDA
Rare	120°F	140°F
Medium-rare	130°F	150°F
Medium	140°F	160°F
Medium-well	150°F	170°F

Beef Roasts	Gourmet	USDA
Rare	125°F	140°F
Medium-rare	135°F	150°F
Medium	145°F	160°F
Medium-well	160°F	170°F

Beef Burgers	Gourmet	USDA
	160°F	160°F +

Lamb Racks	Gourmet	USDA
Rare	125°F	140°F
Medium-rare	135°F	150°F
Medium	145°F	160°F
Medium-well	160°F	170°F

Lamb Chops	Gourmet	USDA
Rare	125°F	140°F
Medium-rare	135°F	150°F
Medium	145°F	160°F
Medium-well	160°F	170°F

Pork Chops	Gourmet	USDA
Medium-well	160°F	--------
Well done	180°F	170°F

Veal Chops	Gourmet	USDA
Medium-rare	135°F	--------
Medium	145°F	150°F
Medium-well	160°F	160°F

Whole Chicken	Gourmet	USDA
	170°F	180°F

Whole Turkey	Gourmet	USDA
	170°F	180°F

Doneness of meat should always be determined using an instant-read meat thermometer inserted in the thickest part of the meat and away from the bone.

While USDA temperature guidelines are valuable for food safety, we find them often overdone, especially on the grill. Many restaurants cook to temperatures aligned more with the "gourmet" column shown here. This requires close attention to safe food-handling guidelines.

Rolled Beef Roasts

As with ground meat, surface bacteria may get worked into the center of rolled beef roasts. Therefore, they should be cooked to an internal temperature of 160°F.

Fish

Fish is thoroughly cooked when it turns opaque and the meat flakes cleanly under firm pressure.

Shrimp and Lobster Tails

Shrimp and lobster are fully cooked with the flesh turns opaque.

Recipes Index

Recipes Index

Recipes Index

Ingredients Index

Ingredients Index

Ingredients Index

Ingredients Index

About Kalamazoo Outdoor Gourmet

Our tradition of superior design and craftsmanship dates back to 1906.

Over a century of sheet metal fabrication expertise is the foundation of Kalamazoo Outdoor Gourmet's superior construction. The secret behind our innovation is the union between our passion for outdoor cooking and our fiercely independent design philosophy.

Innovation is at the heart of every Kalamazoo product. Each part of the collection — from grills and pizza ovens to refrigeration and cabinetry — represents a significant departure from the established norm. Consequently, our list of exclusives and innovations speaks for itself.

The First Hybrid Fire Grills The convenience of gas with the flavor and cooking experiences of charcoal and wood. No other grills seamlessly marry these qualities.

The First *Real* Outdoor Refrigerators Not all outdoor refrigerators are safe for storing raw chicken, but a Kalamazoo is. Our outdoor freezers and freezer drawers are still the only units of their kind. They can even keep ice cream frozen in desert heat thanks to advanced insulation, forced-air cooling and a powerful, variable-speed compressor.

The First Weather-Tight Cabinetry Ours is the only line of cabinets that can keep their contents clean and dry no matter the weather. The seamless rain gutter around every door and drawer opening means you can even hose the kitchen clean—a great advantage for outdoor kitchens exposed to salt spray.

The First Countertop Pizza Oven with Dual-Burner Control The Artisan Fire Pizza Oven allows you to perfectly balance the crisping of the crust and the browning of the toppings.

The First Custom Laser-Cut Cooking Surfaces Only Kalamazoo offers chefs the option of specifying their ideal combination of cooking patterns. Stainless steel surfaces feature unique designs for cooking meat, fish or vegetables (the latter sized so asparagus and green beans can't fall through)—and can even be personalized with monograms or other artwork.

The First High-Performance Stainless Steel Grill with an Offset Smoker Box Traditional, Southern-style smoking isn't possible with just any grill, and that includes most of the stainless steel models out there. Add an offset smoker box to a Kalamazoo and expand its already substantial cooking capabilities.

These are just a few highlights. Visit *KalamazooGourmet.com* to learn more about the host of innovations that distinguish our products.

Search *Kalamazoo Outdoor Gourmet* on YouTube® to watch behind the scenes as our skilled craftspeople build a Kalamazoo Hybrid Fire Grill in Kalamazoo, Michigan.